# Business Productivity Tools

## Excel, PowerPoint, Graphics, and More

**Mike Splane**
*San Jose State University*

**KENDALL/HUNT PUBLISHING COMPANY**
4050 Westmark Drive      Dubuque, Iowa 52002

# Contents

# Introduction

This book is based on my experiences teaching Microsoft Office applications to over 2000 students at San Jose State University. When I started teaching, I was not satisfied with the textbooks that were available to me. They were too expensive for a short course. They contained materials that were either too advanced or too basic for the typical student. The content didn't allow for much interaction between the instructor and the student, consisting mainly of self-paced activities unrelated to practical business-related tasks. And they were not useful as reference material; the students could not find answers to their "How do I do?" questions. I thought I could do better.

The result is this textbook. It includes dozens of practical tips to greatly decrease the time spent performing everyday tasks. It teaches how to use graphics to create beautiful documents, charts, and presentations. It also serves as a reference guide to quickly find out how to perform everyday tasks in Word and Internet Explorer.

# Benefits

The book was created to match the needs of a typical college student, with its content based on my own experiences, both as a student and as an instructor, and on the responses to several hundred student surveys. Because my students come from many different countries, cultures, and backgrounds, I've tried to use clear and simple words to make sure the ideas easily accessible. Each chapter in the textbook covers a set of related skills within a single application.

Typically, students already know how to operate a computer and perform basic tasks in Word. They have grown up with Internet Explorer. Therefore, chapters discussing these applications contain no explanatory text, focusing instead on shortcuts and graphics, and on exploring the use of some less familiar features. These chapters are mainly useful as reference guides.

By contrast, most students are far less familiar with other Office applications. The Excel portion of the book starts with chapters covering the basics. Later chapters gradually get more complex. Shortcuts are included in these chapters too, but the main focus is on clear explanations of fundamentals, backed up by multiple practice assignments.

Two graphic mediums, PowerPoint and Excel Charts, have their own chapters. In business it is not enough to have a good idea. You also need to sell your idea by presenting it in a professional and creative manner. You'll learn how to make presentations that stand out from the crowd, drawing attention that could help to boost your career.

In order to keep prices down, color has not been used in the printing of this book. Where the use of color has been necessary to illustrate a design element, links have been provided to a textbook website. Updates, graphics files, and Excel files that accompany the text are also posted here: *www.cob.sjsu.edu/Bus91L/TextBook*.

# CHAPTER 1

# Word Graphics

This chapter focuses on methods of using Word to create graphics and to perform hidden, interesting, non-routine, or complex tasks relating to graphics.

## Part One   Tables

### Creation and Manipulation of Tables

**To create a table:** Table menu, Insert Table, select the number of rows and columns. Choose an auto-format style. The last three auto-format table styles are designed for use in web-pages.

**To create a space (blank line) above a table:** Click in the top left cell. Press Ctrl + Shift-Enter.

**To select the table:** Use the icon that appears in the upper left corner.

**To align a table:** Select the table (click the icon in upper left corner of the table), then use the alignment icons on the Formatting toolbar.

**To resize the table:** Move the cursor below the lower right corner. An icon appears. Click and drag.

### Changing the Interior Layout of Tables

**To add a row:** Move the cursor into the lower right-hand cell and hit tab.

**To add columns and rows:** From the Table menu, select Insert.

**To remove columns and rows:** From the Table menu, select Delete.

**To merge cells in a table:** Highlight the cells. From the Table menu, select Merge Cells.

**To split cells in a table:** Highlight the cells. From the Table menu select Split Cells.

**To resize column widths:** Click and drag on the cell border, or on the ruler. To have the other columns automatically adjust, hold Ctrl + when dragging the cell border.

### Formatting Tables

**In general:** Use Tables menu, Properties submenu, or the Tables toolbar, to control formatting.

**To control alignment and appearance of text and borders in the table:** Use the Tables menu, Table Properties submenu. Formatting icons work in individual cells, and with groups of highlighted cells.

**To vertically align column labels:** Highlight cells. From the Format menu, select Text Direction. Note: this won't work for files saved as web pages. Try using word art instead.

**To repeat column labels:** From the Table menu, select Heading Rows Repeat.

**To fit text to a cell:** Highlight the desired cells. From the Table menu, Properties submenu, Cell tab, Select Options, Select Wrap Text and Fit Text.

**To clear all text from a table:** Select the table. Press the Delete key.

**To add borders or shading to a table:** Select the table. Right click. Click borders and shadings.

**To create dual shading effects:** Select the cells. First apply shading to a "cell." Then apply a different shading to a "paragraph." This will work with both patterns and fill colors.

**To create customized cell borders:** From the Tables and Borders toolbar. Select a Line Style and weight. Use the border colors "Pencil" to highlight lines in the table.

### Miscellaneous Tips for Tables

**Convert a table to text and vice versa:** From the Table menu, use the Convert submenu.

**Convert tables to spreadsheets and vice versa:** Simply copy and paste from one application into another. Use an area with the same number of columns and rows. Adjust the column width.

**To create a chart from a table:** Select the Table. From the Insert menu, Picture submenu, select Chart. To alter the chart, double or triple click on any screen element. Select Format.

**To add formulas to a table:** Highlight the cell where you want the formula. From the Table menu, select Formula. =SUM(ABOVE) or =SUM(LEFT) will add columns or rows of cells. If summing a series of rows, insert the =SUM(LEFT) command starting from the bottom row and working up.

## Part Two    Working with the Drawing Toolbar

**To turn off the drawing canvas feature (RECOMMENDED):** Tools menu, Options, General tab, deselect "Automatically create drawing canvas when inserting AutoShapes." The manual method is to press Escape whenever the drawing canvas rectangle appears in your document.

**Open the drawing toolbar:** The Drawing toolbar has three parts. The left part is used to manipulate graphics. The center part is used to insert graphics. The right part formats them.

### Working With Lines and Shapes

Lines and Arrows

**To create a line or arrow:** From the Drawing toolbar, click on the line or arrow icon. Click on the spot where you want your line to start. Drag with the mouse. Release the mouse.

**To add a horizontal line graphic:** Format menu, Borders and Shading submenu, Horizontal Line button. Or, from the Drawing toolbar, hold down Shift then press the line icon. Draw your line. Release Shift.

**To add a bend to a line:** On the Drawing toolbar, select the pull down box next to the word Draw. Select Edit Points. Click on a line at the point where you want to bend it and drag. This works with curves too.

**To change the alignment, direction, or length of a line:** Click on an endpoint of the line. Drag.

**To change a line's color, thickness or style:** First create the line. Then use the icons on the toolbar.

**To change arrow points:** Click on an arrow. Click on the arrowhead icon on the Drawing toolbar.

## Shapes

**To create shapes automatically:** Click on AutoShapes. Select a shape. Click in your workspace and draw an area for your graphic.

**To create perfect circles or squares:** Use the Drawing toolbar. Hold down Shift then press the oval or rectangle icon. Draw your shape. Release Shift.

**To quickly copy (replicate) a graphic:** Select the object. Hold Ctrl. Drag and release. Release Ctrl. Alternatively, select the graphic and press Ctrl + D.

## Controlling Spacing

**To evenly space graphics:** Select the graphic and press Ctrl + D. Drag the second graphic the desired distance. Press Ctrl + D as often as desired.

**To align objects horizontally or vertically:** Select the objects as above. On the Drawing toolbar, select Draw. Select Align or Distribute. Select horizontally or vertically.

**To rotate an object:** Click on the object. Click on the green circle and drag.

**To gently nudge a graphic into place:** Hold the Control Key while pressing an arrow key. Using just the arrow key also moves the graphic, but nudges it farther.

**To center a graphic:** Hold Control while selecting and inserting the shape.

**To turn on gridlines:** This is an option under Draw on the Drawing toolbar. You can attach objects to the grid.

## Altering Shapes

**To convert several graphics into one large graphic object:** Press Ctrl while selecting a set of graphics with the mouse. (Alternatively, use the large white arrow on the Drawing toolbar to draw a rectangle around your graphics.) Right click. Select Grouping.

**To change a grouped object into its parts:** Select the object, right click and select Ungroup.

**To adjust the form of a shape:** Select the object. If a yellow handle appears click and drag on it.

**To change a shape into a different shape:** Select the object. From the Drawing toolbar, select Draw, then Change AutoShape. Select a new shape.

Formatting Shapes

**To format an object:** Double click on it. You can alter line styles and add fill effects to graphics.

**To format graphics and shapes from the toolbar:** Use the line style or dash style icon to change lines in shapes. The Shading and 3-D effects icons will add depth to your shape. The Fill Color, Font Color and Line Color icons work with most graphics.

**To add fill effects to graphics and shapes:** Right click. Select Format. On the colors and lines tab, select the pull down box next to Color. Select fill effects from the drop down box.

**To add shadowing or 3-D effects:** Select the object. Left-Click on the Shadowing or 3-D icon. You can add effects to most graphics.

**To create a poster-like font within callouts and labels:** Select the Arial Black font and Bold it.

## Word Art

**To add Word Art:** Left-Click on Word Art, select a style, and then type in your message.

**To wrap text around Word Art:** Select Word Art, Right-Click, Format Word Art, Layout tab.

**To alter the format of Word Art:** Click on the Word Art and use the Word Art toolbar. You can add fill effects, change shapes, change font spacing, and change line style to create your own distinctive styles. Try it. It's fun!

## Text Boxes and Text

**To insert a text box:** A text box is a rectangular AutoShape. Left-Click on the text box icon. Click and drag to shape the dimensions of your text box. You can insert text, pictures, Word Art and clip art inside text boxes.

**To select a text box:** Click on the text in the box. The mouse turns into an I-beam. Press Escape. Now just the text box is selected. Format changes applied to a text box affect all of its contents.

**To add text to AutoShape graphics:** Right click. Select Edit Text. This is useful for callouts and arrows.

**To add a caption to a picture:** Insert a text box over the picture. Enter the caption in the text box. From the Format menu select AutoShapes. On the colors and lines tab, set the Fill color to no color. Set the Fill line color to No-line.

## Pictures, Organization Charts, and Diagrams

Pictures

**To insert a picture:** Click on the Insert Picture icon.

**To move pictures and graphics within a document:** Double Click on the graphic. Click on the Layout tab. Set wrapping style to any style except "In line with text." Click and drag the picture. If you need to fine-tune the graphic's location, hold Alt while dragging. Or use the next tip.

**To change dimensions while resizing a picture:** Right click on it. From the Format Picture submenu, click the size tab. Uncheck the "lock aspect ratio" box.

**To add a border to a graphic or picture:** Double Click on the graphic. Click on the Colors and Lines tab. Select a line color, weight, and style.

**To create an unusual shape for a graphic or picture:** Insert an AutoShape that is a non-solid outline. Right click on the AutoShape. Select Add Text. Paste your graphic.

## Clip Art

**To insert Clip Art:** Click on the Insert Clip Art icon. Enter a topic in Search For. Click GO.

## Charts and Diagrams

**To insert an Organization Chart:** Turn off the drawing canvas. Select the Insert Diagram icon. You can also insert an Organization Chart from the Insert menu under Pictures.

**To modify an Organization Chart:** Turn on the Organization Chart toolbar. You can alter the chart's appearance with the Auto-format icon, alter the layout, add or subtract boxes, or change the lines. To change the lines, click on select, then click on "all connecting lines," then select line color or shapes from the Drawing toolbar. Each box on the chart is an Auto-shape, so you can create a unique format for the backgrounds and text of each box.

**To add a professional-looking diagram:** Select the Insert Diagram icon. Choose one of the five types. You can also insert a diagram from the Insert menu. Use the Diagramming toolbar to change the chart's appearance with the Auto-format icon. Use the Diagramming toolbar to add additional diagram elements, or to change the diagram type.

# Drawing Toolbar

Create a document using Drawing toolbar elements. Before you start, turn on the Drawing toolbar (View menu, Toolbars submenu). Then turn off the drawing canvas: From the Tools menu, Options submenu, General tab, uncheck the box next to "automatically create drawing canvas when inserting AutoShapes." To view an example, go to *www.cob.sjsu.edu/BUS91L/Textbook/CH2Pics.htm.*

1. Create a Banner AutoShape. Type your name as text inside the banner. On a second line, type your section number. *(Hint: Right click on the banner and select Add text.)* Center the text.

2. Add a fill effect to the banner. (Hint: Select the banner, not the text. Right click. Look under Format, Colors and Lines tab, Fill section, select Color and pull down to find the fill effects option.)

3. Add a shadow effect to the banner. (Hint: This is an icon on the toolbar.)

4. Below the banner, create a logo for Java Juice using a combination of at least 4 AutoShapes, lines, rectangles or ovals.

5. Group the shapes so they form a single shape.

6. Add Clip Art or a picture of a potential Java Juice patron. (Hint: Insert the clip art then format its Layout as Square. Then click and drag it to the area to the right of your logo.)

7. Add a callout AutoShape of a thought balloon next to the patron. Add some text to the callout.

8. Group the callout and the clip art. Format the layout as Square and right-aligned.

9. Move to the bottom of the page and insert a page break. (Hint: Deselect the clip art with Ctrl + Space. Enter. Ctrl + Enter.)

10. Insert an organization chart for your company. List yourself as the CEO. List three classmates as officers. (Note: If your version of Word doesn't have an "Insert Diagram or Org Chart" icon on the drawing toolbar, create an Org Chart using drawing toolbar shapes, and use a one-color gradient to fill in the backgrounds. Skip #11.)

11. Change the Layout of the chart to "Beveled Gradient." (Hint: Use the AutoFormat icon on the Organization Chart toolbar.)

12. Below the organization chart, using Word Art, enter the phrase "Key Market Segments." Press Enter a few times to move the Word Art down the page. From the Word Art toolbar, change the shape of the Word Art, change the spacing of the characters, and change the format—use a fill effect.

13. Below the Word Art, insert a Venn diagram. Add an extra circle to the diagram. Click and drag on the resizing handles to make the diagram smaller. Drag the diagram so it fits on the same page as the Word Art. (Note: If your version of Word doesn't have an "Insert Diagram or Org Chart" icon on the drawing toolbar, create the Venn diagram using drawing toolbar shapes, and use a one-color gradient to fill in the backgrounds.)

14. Do NOT enter any descriptive text directly into the Venn diagram.

15. After you have created the Venn Diagram, add four text boxes to the diagram.

16. Enter the name of a market segment in each text box: Students, Retirees, Office Workers, Couples. (Hint: You may have to expand the text boxes.) Add shadow style 17 to the textboxes.

**Save the file. Print out a hardcopy of the assignment to hand in.**

# CHAPTER 2

# Word Tips and Tricks

This chapter focuses on methods of using Word to a) quickly perform routine operations and b) perform hidden, interesting, non-routine, or complex tasks.

## Part One    General Information

### Annoying Features

I like to turn off several features in Word for Office 2003 that I find annoying. Here's how:

**Automatic Bulleted lists:** Use the Tools menu, AutoCorrect, AutoFormat While Typing tab. Uncheck the box.

**Automatic Numbered lists:** Use the Tools menu, AutoCorrect, AutoFormat While Typing tab. Uncheck the box.

**Reading View at Start Up:** Use the Tools menu, Options, General tab. Uncheck the box for Allow Reading Layout at Start Up.

**Reviewing Toolbar at Start Up:** Use the Tools menu, Customize, Toolbars tab. Uncheck the Reviewing Toolbar box. Click Reset.

**Task Panes at Start Up:** Use the Tools, Options, View tab. Uncheck the Startup Task Pane box.

**Office Assistant:** Right click on the assistant. Click on Options. On the Options tab, uncheck the Use Office Assistant box. Click OK.

**Drawing Canvas:** Use the Tools menu, Options, General tab. Uncheck the box for Automatically create drawing canvas. (It interferes with many graphics operations.)

**Smart Tags:** Use the Tools, Options, View tab. Uncheck the Smart Tags box.

**Main Toolbars sharing one row:** Click and drag one toolbar to another row or use the Tools menu, Customize, Options tab.

**Incomplete Menus:** Double click when opening a menu, or use the Tools, Customize, Options tab to permanently fix this.

**Track Changes:** Use the Tools menu, Track Changes. Toggle On/Off. The Reviewing toolbar opens automatically but doesn't close automatically.

**Margin Indicators in Print Layout View:** These are a result of having language support installed for East Asian Languages. To uninstall this add-in, Click on the Start Icon in Windows, Choose Programs/Microsoft Office/Microsoft Office Tools/ Microsoft Office 2003

Language Settings. In the dialog box, select and click remove for Japanese, Chinese, and Korean. Restart.

### Menus and Toolbars

**To show Standard and Formatting toolbars on two rows:** Use the Tools menu, Customize submenu, Options tab. Select "Show Standard and Formatting Toolbars on two rows." Then select "Show full menus." Next, select "Show ScreenTips on toolbars." Finally, select "Show shortcut keys in ScreenTips." Click on Close.

**To add/hide icons on toolbars:** Use the toolbar options pull-down menu at the right end of the toolbar. You can click and drag icons from one menu to another by holding the Alt Key. Don't do this in the computer lab!!!

**To return to the default settings:** Use the Tools menu, Customize, Toolbars tab. Select the toolbar. Click on reset. Click OK.

**To show full menus:** Use the Tools, Customize, Options tab.

**To show ScreenTips on toolbars:** Use the Tools, Customize, Options tab.

**To increase the size of the icons:** Use the Tools, Customize, Options tab.

**To show shortcut keys in ScreenTips:** Use the Tools, Customize, Options tab.

**To show additional toolbars:** From the View menu, select Toolbars. Toggle the toolbar on/off.

**To show different views:** From the View menu, select a View. Views also can be selected from the icons in the lower left hand corner of the document.

**To open or close multiple toolbars simultaneously:** Right click in gray toolbars background.

**To change the default toolbars that appear at startup:** Right click in gray toolbars background. Click Customize. On the toolbars tab select or deselect toolbars. Reset button.

**To move or resize toolbars:** Left-click on the toolbar and drag it.

**To add or remove commands from a menu:** Use the Tools menu, Customize submenu, and select the Commands tab. Select a menu, then click and drag a command.

**To hide toolbars and frames:** From the View menu, select Full Screen.

**To use a pre-existing template:** Use the File menu, select New. In Word 2000 the Templates menu appears automatically. Under Office XP a "New Document" Pane will appear. Select General Templates.

**To split the screen into two views:** Drag on the rectangle at the top of the vertical scroll bar. This can also be done from the Window menu.

**To resize the Task Pane:** Click on the border and drag. You can move the task pane! Click on upper left corner and drag. Not recommended.

## Part Two   Handling Text

### Working with the Mouse

**To select a word:** Double Left-Click on the word.

**To select any amount of text:** Drag over the text.

**To select a row of text:** Move the pointer into the margin, left of the line. Click.

**To select multiple rows of text:** Move the pointer into the margin, left of the line. Click and drag.

**To select a sentence:** Ctrl + Left-Click on the sentence.

**To select a paragraph:** Triple Left-Click in the paragraph, or double click in the left margin.

**To select multiple paragraphs:** Double click in the left margin. Drag up or down.

**To select a block of text:** Click at your starting point. Scroll down. Shift-Click at your end point.

**To select an entire document:** Triple Left-Click in the margin, or type Ctrl + A.

**To select multiple blocks of text:** Highlight the first block of text. Hold down Control, then use the mouse to highlight additional blocks of text. Release Control.

**To select a vertical column of text:** Put your cursor to the left of the column. Hold down the ALT key. Highlight the area. Useful for editing > symbols out of email, removing numbering.

**To access a shortcut menu:** Select something then Right-Click.

**To find synonyms:** Right-Click on the word.

**To edit misspellings:** Misspelled words have red underlines. Right-click and make a selection.

## Short Cut Keys

**To access a shortcut menu:** Select. Press Shift-F10. This simulates right-clicking a mouse.

**Cut, Copy, and Paste:** Ctrl + X, Ctrl + C, Ctrl + V.

**Select the entire document:** Ctrl + A.

**Use the Office Clipboard:** Ctrl + C twice. First position the cursor in the document, then select an item from the clipboard to paste it. You can access the clipboard from the Task Pane drop-down list, or from the Edit menu, Office Clipboard.

**Go to the beginning or end of the document:** Ctrl + Home or Ctrl + End.

**Create a line across the page:** On a new line type one of these six symbols: ~ - _ * = #. Repeat twice more, and then press Enter. Each symbol gives you a different type of line (wavy, single, bold, dotted, double, or triple).

**To remove a line:** Select the paragraph above it. Press Ctrl + Q.

**Insert a page break:** Press Ctrl + Enter.

**To find synonyms:** Press Shift + F7.

**Increase font size for an entire document:** Select the whole document (Ctrl + A) then press Ctrl + ] as many times as desired. Each click increases the font size by one point.

**Decrease font size for an entire document:** Select the whole document (Ctrl + A) then press Ctrl + [ as many times as desired. Each click decreases the font size by one point.

**To double space lines in a paragraph:** Select the paragraph. Ctrl + 2. Use Ctrl + 1 to reverse the procedure. Use Ctrl + 5 to set the distance between lines to 1.5 spaces. Note: this doesn't work with the numeric keypad keys.

**Align Right, Left, Center, Justify:** Ctrl + R, Ctrl + L, Ctrl + E, Ctrl + J.

**Indent and Decrease Indent:** Ctrl + M or Shift-Ctrl + M.

**Find/Replace:** Ctrl + F or F5. Type in the word you are looking for.

**Select a Table:** Click in a cell. Alt-F5.

**Open a document:** Ctrl + O.

**Open a new document:** Ctrl + N.

**Print the document:** Ctrl + P.

**Save the file:** Ctrl + S (or F12 to Save As).

**Create a Hyperlink:** Ctrl + K.

**Undo, Redo:** Ctrl + Z, Ctrl + Y.

**Selecting Text:** Press F8 repeatedly. Or press F8 then use arrow keys. Press Escape to turn off.

**Selecting Blocks of Text:** Position the cursor in a word. Hold down control and use the arrow keys, the PageUp PageDown keys, or the Home and End keys.

**Add a Date or Time field that updates automatically:** Alt-Shift-D, Alt-Shift-T.

### Moving Around the Document

**To search for text:** Press F5 or Ctrl + F.

**To move to sections listed in a Table of Contents:** Hold down Control then click on the heading.

**To jump quickly around the document:** Press F5 for options.

**To move to previous cursor locations:** Use Shift + F5.

**To create bookmarks:** Position the cursor at the location where you want a bookmark. From the Insert menu, select Bookmark. Enter the Bookmark name.

**To move to a bookmark:** Use the F5 key and select from the pull-down list of bookmarks.

**To search for non-text items:** Click the circular icon below the vertical scroll bar. Choose the type of object you want to look for. Use the up or down browse buttons on the vertical scroll bar to quickly search the document.

## Part Three    Formatting and Working With Text

### Paragraphs and Spacing

**To set indents for paragraphs:** Use the Format menu, Paragraph submenu, Indents and Spacing tab to set indentations to an exact distance. Positive numbers make the text area narrower, negative numbers widen the text area. Alternative methods are to use the Indent/Decrease icons on the toolbar, or click and drag on the polygons on the horizontal ruler.

**To widen the space between characters:** Format menu, Font submenu, Character Spacing tab.

**To widen the space between paragraphs:** Format menu, Paragraph submenu, Indents and Spacing tab. Character Spacing section, increase the number of pts.

**To have right and left aligned text on the same line:** Put the cursor at the beginning of the line. From the Format menu, Tabs submenu, type 6" (this is the right-hand margin setting, in inches) as the "tab stop position." Select right alignment then OK. Enter text on the left hand side. Press tab. Enter text.

**To create newspaper-style columns for text:** Select the paragraph or area you want to appear in columns. From the format menu, choose Columns. You can add lines between columns here. Use the horizontal ruler to adjust spacing between columns.

**To create hyphenated text:** Tools menu, Language submenu, Hyphenation submenu, check Automatically Hyphenate Document.

**To change the underline color or shape:** Format menu, Paragraphs submenu.

**Remove the underline from a hyperlink:** Select the link. Double-Click the underline icon.

**To quickly change the letter case:** Shift-F3 cycles through different options or use the Format menu.

**To reset paragraph format to the default:** Ctrl + Q.

## Special Characters

**For superscript and subscript formatting:** You can add icons to the Formatting toolbar. The keyboard shortcuts are Ctrl + = for subscripts and Ctrl + Shift = for superscripts. Repeat the keystrokes to turn the formatting off.

**To insert a symbol or character:** Use the Insert menu, Symbol submenu. Scroll to find your symbol. Highlight it and press insert. Continue selecting symbols. Click close when finished. The font size and color of symbols can be changed after you insert it. For older versions of Word, look under Start Programs > Accessories > System Tools.

**To create a dropped cap:** Use the Format menu, Dropped Cap option.

**To create small caps:** Highlight text. Format menu, Font submenu. Small caps are capital letters shrunk to the same height as lowercase, mainly used for emphasis. This won't work for web pages.

## Styles

**To quickly format text:** Apply a style from the style pull-down box on the Formatting toolbar.

**About master styles:** Normal is the default style. Body Text style is like Normal except it adds a 6 point (half a line) spacing below each paragraph. Web is for use with Web Pages. Headings 1, 2, and 3 are useful for automatically creating outlines and table of contents. Changes to these master styles will automatically change any sub-styles that are derived from these master styles.

**To create a sub-style:** Changes you make with the formatting menu or icons will automatically generate sub-styles.

**To modify a master style:** Formatting Styles: on the Format menu, click Styles and Formatting. Word will display the Styles and Formatting task pane. Right click the name of the style, and choose Modify.

**To remove a style:** Click the double A symbol left of the style box. Select a style then click on the down arrow. Select delete. Note: Any text using the deleted style will revert to "normal" style.

**To duplicate and copy styles:** Use the paintbrush icon. Left-Click anywhere on the font style you want to copy. Left-click on the paintbrush icon. Your cursor becomes a paintbrush. Paint the area where you want to apply the original style. If you want to copy the style to multiple areas, double click on the paintbrush and press Esc when finished.

### Bullets and Lists

**To change bullet or numbering styles:** First create the bullets or numbering in your document using the icon on the Formatting toolbar. This is an on/off toggle switch. From the Format menu, choose Bullets and Numbering.

**To create multi-level bullets:** Type in all of the bullets, including sub-points. Highlight and click the bullets icon. Highlight the lines you want as sub-bullets and press the indent icon.

**Another way is to select a bulleted list:** From the Format menu, Bullets submenu, choose the Outline Numbered tab.

**To widen line spacing in numbered lists:** Select the list. Press Ctrl + zero.

### Borders and Shadings

**To create artistic page borders for a document:** From the Format menu, Borders and Shading submenu, Page Border tab, select Custom and Art. Select a design. Change the "width" and "apply to" options if desired.

**To add a border to text:** Format menu, Borders and Shading submenu, Border tab. You have a choice of line colors, patterns, and widths.

**To add a fill color to text:** Format menu, Borders and Shading submenu, Shading tab. Select a color from the Fill area of the dialog box. Leave the Patterns style as "Clear." Make a selection from the "Apply to" box.

**To add shading or a pattern to text:** Use the Format menu, Borders and Shading submenu, Shading tab. Select a style from the Patterns area of the dialog box, then select a color from the Patterns area (lower left pull-down box). Important: Leave the fill color set to "No Fill." Make a selection from the "Apply to" box. Enter.

### Miscellaneous

**To automatically create a table of contents:** Set the "style" of all references wanted in the Table of Contents to heading level 1, 2, or 3. From the Insert menu, select Reference, then Index and Tables, then use the Table of Contents tab.

**To edit heading styles:** You can use the Outline View to quickly edit heading styles.

**To allow direct clicking on links:** Tools menu, Options, Edit tab. Uncheck "Use Ctrl + Click..."

**To compare two documents side-by-side:** Open both documents. Select from Window menu.

**To create an Executive Summary:** Tools menu, pick Auto Summarize. Choose an option.

**To check word count:** Tools menu, Word Count. The Word Count toolbar has more features.

**To create a re-usable text template:** Create the text in word. Highlight the text. Drag it onto the desk top. Copy it into other documents whenever it is needed.

**To repeat a word or series of letters:** Type the word then Press F4. Example: ChaChaCha.

**To translate into French or Spanish:** Select Text. Tools menu, Language submenu, Translate.

**To insert a footnote or endnote:** Position the cursor where you want the marker to appear in the text. On the Insert menu, Reference submenu, select Footnote. In the Location box, choose either endnote or footnote and press Enter. Word will 1) display a marker in the body of your text where your cursor was positioned and 2) reposition the cursor at the bottom of the page in a special area for entering the citation. Type in the citation in that bottom area or, if citing from a website, copy and paste the web address to that area. The footnote/endnote area should never contain any graphics.

## Part Four    Printing and Files

### *Printing*

**Centering documents vertically:** File, Page Setup, Layout, Page, select from the pull-down box.

**Previewing the document before printing:** Use the print preview icon on the standard toolbar.

**To edit a document in Print Preview:** Click the Magnifier button. Zoom in. You can use keyboard shortcuts, but not the mouse, to edit. Click the magnifier icon when finished editing.

**To add a header or footer:** From the View menu, select Header and Footer. A toolbar opens. You can toggle between header and footer. Press the close icon when finished.

**To apply a header to just the first page:** From the View menu, select Header and Footer. A toolbar opens. Click the Page Setup icon. On the layout tab, select Different First Page. Type the header. Press the close icon when finished.

**To add page numbers:** From the Insert menu in Normal View or Print Layout View. Or use the View menu, Header and Footer submenu.

**To change the starting page number on a document:** From the Insert menu, select Page Numbers, then Left-Click on the Format button.

**To add a watermark:** From the Print Layout View. Format menu, Background submenu, Printed Watermark. Click on picture or text. Select a picture or enter a text message. Choose formatting. The watermark will not appear in the web view, or on a webpage.

**To print "Tracked Changes":** From the File menu, Print submenu, Print what box, select Document showing markup. To stop printing the changes, choose Document.

**To get rid of a short last page:** Print preview, "Shrink to Fit" Icon. To reverse: Edit menu, Undo.

## *File Management*

**To reduce file size when emailing:** Save it as Rich Text Format.

**To create a PowerPoint Presentation from a Word document:** Use the File menu, Send to submenu, Microsoft Office PowerPoint. All text formatted in Heading 1 Style will show up as PowerPoint Slides. Text formatted as Heading 2 and 3 Styles will show up as bullet points.

**To create a webpage as a single file:** Choose File Save-as Single File Web Page. This puts all of your graphics and fonts into a single file. If you save as a webpage, graphics are stored as separate files inside a folder and you have to upload both the file and the folder to your server.

**To find a lost file:** File menu, Open, Click on Tools, Search, Advanced tab. Select a property. Enter search parameters.

# Essay Assignment

### Section One – Short Story or Essay

1.  The first section of your paper will be a short story about yourself, a classmate, or a business topic. The essay should be 3–4 paragraphs long and contain about 300–600 words. The story should be spaced at 1.5 lines. The paragraph alignment style should be "justified." The font size should be 11 or 12 points.

2.  Do NOT submit a paper you have written for another class.

3.  This section should be preceded with a title (heading). For example: About Me.

4.  Use the "Style" box on the Formatting toolbar to apply a "Heading 1" style to the title.

5.  Underneath the title, insert a copyright symbol followed by your name and the year. A shortcut to create the symbol is to type a c in parentheses.

6.  Change the first letter in the essay to a dropped cap. This option is on the Format menu.

### Section Two – Links

1.  Underneath the story about yourself, type a heading "My Favorite Links."

2.  Use the "Style" box on the Formatting toolbar to apply a "Heading 3" style to this heading.

3.  Enter 3–6 hyperlinks, one per line. Ctrl + K is a shortcut to create a hyperlink.

4.  Format the hyperlinks as bullet points.

5.  Change the bullet point symbol. Use the Format menu, Bullets and Numbering submenu.

### Section Three – Quotation

1.  Underneath the Links Section, type a heading "Web Quotation."

2.  Use the "Style" box on the Formatting toolbar to apply a "Heading 3" style to this heading.

3.  Go to the web and find a story about something that interests you. Copy and paste the first paragraph into your document.

4.  Insert an endnote with appropriate citation. (Insert menu, Reference submenu, Footnote.)

5.  After you have pasted the source information into the endnote area, return the cursor to the document area of the worksheet.

### Header and Footer

1.  Create a header containing your name and section number. Headers and Footers are on the View menu. Right align the text.

2.  Add page numbers to the footer. Center them.

### Section Four – Picture

1.  Make sure your cursor is not in the Endnote area. Nothing goes in that part of the document except for author and source information.

2.  Underneath the Quotation, NOT IN THE FOOTNOTE AREA!, type a heading "Image from the Web."

3.  Use the "Style" box on the Formatting toolbar to apply a "Heading 3" style to this heading.

4.  Go to the Google website and find an image that relates to the quotation. Copy and paste the image into your document.

### Above the Short Story – Insert a Table of Contents

1.  When the paper is complete, insert a table of contents. Position your cursor below the line which contains your name and the copyright symbol. (Insert menu, Reference submenu, Index and Tables.)

2.  Under the Table of Contents, use the AutoFormat feature to insert a line. (Example: On a blank line type *** and press enter.) If Word doesn't have this option, create a line using the drawing toolbar.

### Section Five – Word Jeopardy Table

1.  Below the Image and above the endnote area, insert a table. The table should be 4 columns wide and 7 rows deep.

2.  Merge the cells in the top row. Split the first cell in row two into 2 rows and 1 column. Enter text into the cells as shown in the sample table. Make the headings in rows one and two Bold, center them (both vertically and horizontally), and make them 14 point font.

3.  In column 2, rows 3–7, enter words that end with the letters "ough."

4.  In column 3, rows 3–7, enter words that contain the letter Q, but do not start with a Q.

5.  In column 4, rows 3–7, enter words that contain the letter J, but do not start with a J.

6.  Center the text and numbers in rows 3–7.

7.  Add shading to the cells using at least two different colors. (First highlight the cells you want to add color to. Use the Format menu, Borders and Shadings submenu, Shadings tab. Apply to: Cells.)

| Jeopardy | | | |
|---|---|---|---|
| **Words with:**<br>**Score** | **"ough" words** | **"Q" words** | **"J" words** |
| 200 | rough | require | Majestic |
| 400 | tough | acquire | objective |
| 600 | dough | request | adjective |
| 800 | enough | aquarium | adjust |
| 1000 | although | Requisite | Mojave |

**Save the file. Before coming to class, print out a hardcopy of the assignment to hand in.**

# CHAPTER 3

# Introducing Excel

## Beginning Excel

### Identifying the Parts of the Excel Worksheet

- The Workbook Environment is similar to a Tic-Tac-Toe grid, only much bigger.
- Close the Task Pane if it opens when you open Excel.
- Turn on the Standard and Formatting toolbars from the View menu, Toolbars submenu.
- Use the Tools menu, Customize submenu, Options tab to Show toolbars on two rows. Select all options except large icons, and then click Close. You'll see this:

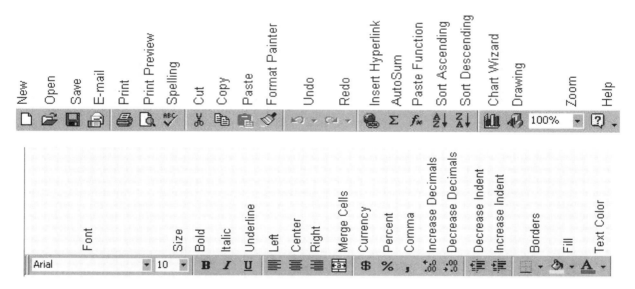

Note the "Currency" icon is mislabeled. It is actually "Accounting" style.

## Moving Around the Worksheet

- Cells have names, consisting of a letter and a number. Select a cell with the mouse and you will see a letter highlighted at the top and a number highlighted on the left.
- The name of the selected cell also appears in the Name Box, above the letter A.
- Tab moves you to the right, Enter moves you down, Shift + Tab moves you to the left.
- Other ways to move around: the Arrow Keys, Home, End, Page Up, Page Down.

- Use the Control key with the arrow keys to extend their effect.
- Typing a cell name in the Name Box moves the cursor into that cell.
- Ctrl + Page Up or Ctrl + Page Down shifts between worksheets.
- Double clicking on a cell wall moves you to the edge of a row or column of data.

### Entering Characters, Dates, and Numeric Data

- Select a cell. Enter text or numbers by typing.
- Or, enter data in the formula bar that is centered directly above the worksheet.
- Enter dates as xx/xx or xx-xx. Enter the year if it differs from the current one.
- Ways to Edit Cell Contents:
  1. Select the cell and then click in the formula bar to edit its contents.
  2. Or, select the cell and type in a new entry.
  3. Or, select the cell; then press F2 to edit directly in the cell.
- Click and Drag to Move Data.
- To Undo / Redo use icons or use shortcut keys: Ctrl + Z and Ctrl + Y.

### Copying Formulas

There are several ways to copy and paste. Use the mouse to highlight the cells that you want to copy from. Do not highlight the formula bar area! That will delete the cell contents!

- Press Ctrl + C. Highlight the area you want to copy the formula into. Press Ctrl + V.
- Click on the Copy icon. Highlight the area you want to copy the formula into. Click on the Paste icon.
- Click on the Copy icon. Highlight the area you want to copy the formula into. Press the Enter key.
- From the Edit menu, select Copy. Highlight the area you want to copy the formula into. From the Edit menu select Paste.
- Move the cursor around until you get a small black cross in the lower right hand corner of the highlighted area. Click and drag (down or across) to highlight the area you want the formula copied into. Release the mouse.

### Making Formatting Changes

- Formatting from the Toolbar
  1. The five Standard Text options. (Font, Size, Bold, Italics Underline.)
  2. Aligning Text and Labels – Icons. (Left, Center, Right, Indent, Decrease Indent.)
  3. Merge/Unmerge Cells Icon. (Toggle Switch.)
  4. Adding Cell Borders and Shading – Icons.
  5. Use icons for Percents, Accounting, or Comma Styles to format numbers.
  6. Use the decimal icons to change the number of decimal places displayed.

- The Format Dialog Box is used to format Cells or Ranges
    1. Select a cell or range of cells. A range is a group of cells forming a rectangle.
    2. To access the dialog box: Right click and choose Format Cells from the menu.
    3. Change the numbering style from the Numbers tab.
    4. Change how letters are displayed within a cell using the Alignment tab.
    5. Change Font Style, Size, and Color from the Font tab.
    6. Add backgrounds with the Borders and Patterns tabs.
- Format Rows and Columns
    1. From the Format menu, you can change the height and width, or hide and unhide.
    2. You can also use the mouse for some tasks.
    3. To change row heights and column widths, click and drag between the row or column indicators.
    4. To fit a column width to the width of its contents, double click between column or row indicators.
- Shortcuts
    1. The AutoFill Handle quickly copies text and formulas:
        a. Position the cursor in the lower right hand corner of a range.
        b. A small + appears. Drag in any direction.
        c. Use AutoFill to enter a series of dates, months or days.
        d. Use AutoFill to extend a series of numbers.
        e. Use AutoFill to copy formulas.
    2. To format large areas: Select letters to format columns, numbers to format rows, or the blank cell above the numbers column to format all.
    3. To copy formatting, select a cell with the desired format. Click the Paintbrush icon. Use the mouse to select the cells, row numbers, or column letters where you want the desired format to be applied.

### AutoSum

- The AutoSum icon ($\Sigma$) gives the sum of a selected column, row, or range.
- For example, the cell containing the formula = SUM(C3:G9) displays the sum of all of the numbers in a rectangle with corners at C3 and G9.
- To use AutoSum, first position the cursor in a cell where you want a total. Then click on the icon. Use the mouse to alter the shape of the range of numbers you want included in your total.
- Or, highlight a column of data (include a blank cell at the bottom). Click on the icon.
- Or, highlight a row of data (include a blank cell at the right). Click on the icon.
- Or, highlight a range, including a column of blank cells to the right and a row of blank cells below the range. Click on the icon to quickly total all the rows and columns.
- Or, position the cursor in a cell where you want a total. Click on the icon. Hold down Control while selecting cells from different areas.

### Validation

- The validation feature is found on the Data menu. You can use all the tabs, any combination of tabs, or a single tab.
- The Settings tab is used to restrict the entry of data to specific types of data.
- The Input Message tab tells users what type of data to enter.
- The Error Alert tab is used to help users when they have made a mistake.
- Validation rules are applied to individual cells.

### Working with Multiple Worksheets

- Click on a worksheet tab to move into a different worksheet.
- By right-clicking on a worksheet tab, you can:
  1. Insert and Delete Worksheets,
  2. Move and Copy Worksheets,
  3. Rename a Worksheet,
  4. Select Multiple Worksheets to work on simultaneously,
  5. Add colors to the tabs.

# Beginning Excel

## Open Excel

From the Tools menu, Customize submenu, Options tab, select all options except "large icons."

From the View menu, close the task pane, if it is open. (Uncheck the box next to it.)

From the View menu, select Toolbars.

Only the Standard and the Formatting toolbars should have checks next to them. Remove any checkmarks next to the other toolbars.

Notice that the menus show icons and shortcut keys next to some of the menu choices. These are alternative ways to perform the same task.

## Moving Around in the Worksheet

The worksheet opens in cell A1. This is called the home cell. Notice that the letter A above it and number 1 to the left of it are highlighted to indicate which cell you are currently working with. There is a thick border around the cell.

1. Use the mouse to click on another cell to select it. Notice how the letter above it and number to the left are highlighted, and the thick border moved.
2. Find the Cell Name in the box in the upper left hand side of the display.
3. Type G6 in the Cell Name Box. Press Enter.
4. Press Tab, Enter, and Shift Tab.
5. Press the arrow keys. Press and hold one down to scroll.
6. Press Page Down to move down one screen. Press Page Up.
7. Press the End key with the down arrow key to move to the bottom of the sheet.
8. Press the End key with the right arrow key to move to the far right column.
9. Press Ctrl + Home to return to Cell A1.

## Formatting Methods

1. Enter letters in cells A1 and B1, numbers in cells A2 and B2.
2. Widen the columns by clicking between letters in the letters row and dragging.
3. Change the height of the rows by clicking in the number area and dragging.
4. Notice that words are left aligned, numbers are right aligned.

5.   Click on Cell A2 and press the centering icon.

6.   Click on the letter B and click on the centering icon.

7.   Click on the number 2 and click on the left alignment icon.

8.   Use the mouse to select cells A1 to B2. Press Delete.

9.   Click on the tab for Sheet 2.

### Build a Small Table

1.   In cell A1 type "Fun Things to do." Press Tab, Enter, or an arrow key.

2.   Click on the letter A. Drag to widen this column.

3.   Click on cell A1 again. Press F2. Change A1 to say "Fun Things To Do."

4.   Press Ctrl + Z to reverse the correction.   *Ctrl + Y: redo*

5.   Click in the formula bar. (The area above the center of the worksheet.)

6.   Change A1 to say Fun Things To Do.

7.   In cells A2-A4, list 3 of your friends.

8.   Select cells A2-A4 by highlighting them with your mouse.

9.   Click on the A-Z icon to sort the names. If the names don't sort correctly, try again, but this time include cell A1.

10.   List an activity in column B next to each name.

11.   Use icons to apply color formatting to the font and background in cell A1.

12.   Click on the number 2 in the row indicator column. Click on the fill color icon.

13.   Select cell A2. Click on the paintbrush icon. Use the mouse to select the numbers 3 and 4.

14.   Use the borders icon to apply a Heavy Border to cell A1.

15.   Select cells A1 and B1. Click the Merge and Center icon. Click the icon twice more.

16.   Press Ctrl + A to select all cells.

17.   Press Ctrl + B to apply Bold format. Press Escape.

**Close Excel**

# Numbers and Formulas

## Working with Numbers

In cells A1-A4, enter the numbers 2,3,4,5. Left click and use your mouse to highlight cells A1 to A4. Release the mouse button. Move the cursor until a tiny + sign appears in the lower right hand corner of cell A4. Click and drag down four rows. The numbers 6,7,8 and 9 should appear. This AutoFill handle is a quick way to extend series of numbers, dates, months, and days of the week. You can use it to copy formulas, too.

Change the 2 in cell A1 to a Currency format. To access the Format dialog box, first select the cell, then either double-click, right-click, press Ctrl + 1, or use the Format menu. Find the Number tab and choose Currency.

Change the format of the 3 in cell A2 by clicking on the $ icon. This icon applies the Accounting format to numbers. It is mislabeled as Currency. The dollar sign displayed in cell A2 is to the far left of the number 3. Look at cell A1 to compare the two formats.

You can use the paintbrush icon to quickly copy formatting into other cells, rows, columns, or worksheets. Click on cell A1. Click on the format painter icon. Click the down arrow. The dollar sign in cell A2 will move next to the 3.

Click on cell A9. Type 7-9 numbers at random and press enter.

Click again in cell A9. Click on the Comma icon.

Railroad tracks ##### may appear. This means the column is too narrow. To fix this problem, widen the column. One way is to move the cursor between the letters A and B and double-click. Another way is to click and drag in the column heading.

With cell A9 selected, Click on the increase decimals and decrease decimals icons to see what happens.

## Formulas

In cell C1, enter the math formula 4 * 7. You may be surprised that the number 28 didn't appear in cell C1. That's because Excel formulas have to start with an arithmetic symbol, usually an = sign.

In cell C2, enter the math formula = 4 * 7. This time you'll see the result of the formula, 28, appear in the cell. Click on C2 and look at the formula bar to see the actual formula. Excel shows formulas in two ways. The actual formula appears in the formula bar. The result of the formula shows in the cell. This is like a flashcard.

In cell C3, enter the formula = 9 / 3.

In cell C4 enter the formula = 5 + 6.

To see all of the formulas in the worksheet, press Ctrl + ~ . This is a toggle switch. One view, what I call mirror view, shows all of the formulas in the worksheet. The other view, flashcard view, shows the results of the calculation in the worksheet. Flashcard view is the default. Mirror view is used for checking formulas. It does not show formatting, and numbers are left aligned. Press Ctrl + ~ to return to flashcard view.

### Use Cell References in Place of the Numbers

Delete the formulas in column C. Select the cells and use the delete key.

In cell C1, enter the formula = 5 + 6.

In cell C2 enter the formula = A4 + 6. In cell C3 enter the formula = A4 + A5.

The results of the calculations in cell C1, C2 and C3 are the same, 11. You can use either numbers or the names of cells containing numbers when you write formulas.

Change the number in cell A4 to 8. Notice that the results displayed in cell C2 and C3 changed to 14. This is what makes Excel both POWERFUL and DANGEROUS. If you use formulas containing cell references, changing a number in one cell could cause other cells to change what they display.

### Copying Formulas into New Cells

Switch to mirror view by pressing Ctrl + ~.

Copy and paste the formula from cell C3 to cell C4. Notice the row numbers in the cell references changed from a 4 and a 5 into a 5 and a 6.

You can quickly copy a formula into a neighboring cell. Click on cell C4. Type Ctrl + C. Press the down arrow key and then Enter. Notice that the row numbers in the formula changed again. This is the default for formulas. If you copy them into a different row, the numbers in any cell references will change. If you copy them into different columns, the letters in any cell references will change.

You can turn this automatic adjustment feature off. Edit the formula in C5 to include a $ in front of one of the row numbers. The $ tells Excel "Don't change the part of the cell reference following this sign when copying this formula." You can use a dollar sign in front of the letter, or the number, or both.

The AutoFill handle can be used to quickly copy formulas. Click on cell C5. Move the cursor until a tiny + sign appears in the lower right hand corner of the cell. Click and drag down over cells C6, C7 and C8. See how one row number changed, and the other didn't.

Copy the contents of cell C2 into cell D2. Notice the A becomes a B.

Edit the formula in cell C3 to include a $ in front of one of the A's.

Copy that formula into cell D3. Notice what happens to the letters.

### Absolute Cell References

Edit the formula in cell C3 to include dollar signs in front of the letters and the numbers. This format, with two dollar signs in the cell reference, is called an absolute cell reference. The cell reference will stay unchanged wherever you copy the formula. Cell references that contain one dollar signed are called mixed cell references. The part without the dollar sign can change in mixed cell references.

Copy this formula into 2 or 3 other cells. Notice that this formula is unchanged.

## *Ranges*

Range notation lets you work with groups of cells.

A range is a rectangular block of cells. A range is described by its two opposite corners, separated by a colon. =SUM is a quick way to add up all the numbers in a range of cells.

Press Ctrl + ~ to switch to flashcard view. Enter numbers in cells D1,D2 D3, E1,E2,E3.

In cell E5 Type =SUM(D1:E3) - a range can be a rectangle shape.

Edit the formula in cell E5 to =SUM(D1:D3) - a range can be a column.

Edit the formula in cell E5 to =SUM(D1:E1) - a range can also be a row.

# Cashier's Report

## *Tasks*

1. In cell A1 type "cashiers." In cell B1 type "Cash Sales." In C1 type "Actual Cash." In D1 type "Over/(Short)." Edit cell A1 to change cashiers to Cashiers. (Press F2, or type directly in the address bar, or type directly in the cell.)

2. In cells A2, A3, A4 enter the names of three people. Use the mouse to select cells A2, A3, and A4. Press the AZ icon to sort the names alphabetically.

3. In cells B2, B3, and B4, enter the numbers 120, 80, and 160. These were the cash register readings. In cells C2, C3, and C4 enter the numbers 125, 80 and 158. This is the amount of cash turned in by the cashiers.

4. Was the amount of cash turned in by the cashiers over or short of the expected amount? If you want Excel to do any calculations, start with an = sign. In cell D2 enter = 125 – 120. In cell D3 enter = 80 – 80. In cell D4 enter = 158 – 160. Look at the results of the formulas in cells D2, D3 and D4. Do the results make sense?

5. What if the cash numbers changed in columns B and C? We would need to use different numbers in the formulas in column D. We don't want to write a new formula every time a number changes in a cell, so we need a shortcut. Instead of using numbers in our formulas, we can use the name of the cell that contains the number. This is called a cell reference. Edit cells D2, D3, and D4 to contain cell references. = C2 – B2, = C3 – B3, = C4 – B4. Did the results displayed in cells D2, D3 and D4 stay the same?

6. Notice that the formulas are not displayed in the worksheet, only the results of the formulas are showing. The actual formula for the selected cell appears in the formula bar above the worksheet. This is the default view, which I call the Flashcard view. If you want to see the formulas in the cell, press Ctrl + ~. This is what I call mirror view, since both the formula bar and the cell display the same information. Mirror view is great when you need to find mistakes in formulas. Press Ctrl + ~ again to return to the flashcard view.

7. In cell A5, enter the word "Totals." In cell B5 enter = 120 + 80 + 160. In cell C5 enter = C2 + C3 + C4. In cell D5 enter =SUM(D2:D4) These are all methods for adding groups of numbers. The last method is the most powerful one. It's designed for working with several cells arranged in a rectangle shape. The shape is called a range. To use a range in a formula, list the first cell in the upper left hand corner of the range, a colon, and then list the cell in the opposite corner.

8. Delete the contents of cell B5. Highlight cells B2, B3, B4, and B5. Press the AutoSum icon. Press Enter. This is a quick way to create the SUM formula to add a column of numbers.

9.  Insert a new column between A and B. In cell B1 type "# of Sales." In cells B2, B3, and B4 enter 25, 21, and 30. Copy the formula from cell D5 into cell B5. Switch to mirror view (Ctrl + ~). What changed in the formula that you copied from cell D5? When you copy a formula from one column to another, the letters in the cell references change by default. Notice that when you inserted the new column B, the cells that contained your old data all shifted one column to the right. Excel automatically adjusted your existing formulas to correct for this.

10. In cell F1 enter "CC Sales." In cell G1 enter "Total Sales" In cell H1 enter "Avg Check." In cells F2, F3 and F4 enter 80, 40, and 120. In cell G2 enter the formula = C2 + F2. Did you get 200? In cell H2 enter the formula = G2 / B2. Did you get 8?

11. Copy the formulas in cells G2 and H2 down into the next 2 rows (into cells G3, G4, H3 and H4). Did the results in column H show decimal places? You can increase or decrease the number of decimal places using icons on the tool bar. Change cells H2, H3 and H4 to show 2 decimal places.

12. Switch to mirror view (Ctrl + ~). What changed in the formulas that you copied from cells G2 and H2? When you copy a formula from one row to another, the numbers in the cell references change by default.

13. Change the format of the data in the "# of Sales" column to Number Style. (Ctrl + 1) Change the format of the Cash column to Currency style. (Use the Format menu.) Use the paintbrush icon to copy the currency style into columns DEFG. Use the "Currency" icon to change the Average Check column to Accounting style. Use the Center icon to center all of the cell contents in columns B through H.

14. Insert a new row 1. Use the merge and center icon to create a heading cell across the top of the first 8 columns. Type "Java Juice – Cashier Report" in the cell. Add a background color to the cell and change the font color. Add a heavy border around the cell.

15. Insert a new row below row 4. Highlight the area from A4 to H4. Copy down into the new row. Use mirror view to examine the new formulas. What changed and why?

16. Use the undo icon (or Ctrl + Z) to reverse the copying. Edit the value of the formulas to include dollar signs before the numbers in the cell references. Copy the formulas down again. What parts of the formulas changed this time? What effect did the dollar signs have?

17. Delete the row (5) that you just added.

18. In cell A8 enter "Date." In cell C8 enter today's date. You can separate the month and day with either a dash or a slash. You do not need to enter the year, unless you want a date to refer to a different year than the current one. 1-15 or 1/15 will both give you January 15th. Dates can also be formatted (Ctrl + 1).

19. In cell A9 enter "Accounting Entry:" Use the Merge and Center icon on cells A9, B9 and C9. In cell A10 enter "Cash (DR)." In cell A11 enter A/R-CC (DR)." In cell A12 enter "Sales Rev (CR)." In cell B11 enter = SUM(A3:A5). In cell B12 enter = SUM(F3:F5). In cell C13 enter = SUM(G3:G5).

20. Use the Accounting Format icon (this is a $; it is mislabeled as Currency) and the Increase Decimal icon to format cell C13 as Accounting style, with 2 decimal places. Use the format paintbrush to copy the format from cell C13 into cells B11 and B12.

21. Change some of the numerical data to see how the formula results change.

# Practicing With Excel Formulas

When you enter a formula into a cell, you see the formula in the "formula bar" above the worksheet. If the formula also appears in the cell, you are in "mirror" view. If the formula does not appear in the cell, you are in "flashcard" view. Switch between the two views by simultaneously pressing Ctrl + ~ on the keyboard. Do this exercise in flashcard view.

Construct the Excel Worksheet as shown.

|   | A | B | C | D |
|---|---|---|---|---|
| 1 | 2 | 3 | 4 | 2 |
| 2 | 5 | 6 | 2 | 12 |
| 3 | 3 | 2 | 5 | 7 |
| 4 |   |   |   |   |
| 5 |   |   | The formula goes here |   |

In the second column of the table, rewrite the formula, replacing cell references with numbers.
Do the math and enter the result in the third column.
Enter the formula into cell C5. Check your prediction with what is displayed.
If you understand the formula, move to the next formula and repeat the same steps.

=SUM(A1:B3) asks for the sum of six cells in the rectangle with A1 and B3 as opposite corners.
The ^ sign indicates an exponent. = A3 ^ 2 asks you to square the number stored in cell A3.

| Formulas | Replace the cell references in the formulas with numbers | Do the math | Enter the formula into cell C5. What does Excel show? |
|---|---|---|---|
| = B3 + A3 | Example: = 2 + 3 | 5 | 5 |
| = B2 * C1 | | | |
| = C3 – C2 | | | |
| = B2 + B3 + C3 | | | |
| = B1 + 7 | | | |
| = 5 + C3 | | | |
| = C3 * 8 | | | |
| = D2 / 4 | | | |
| = D2 * D3 | | | |
| = D2 * D3 / D1 | | | |
| = C3 * .4 | | | |
| = C3 * 1.6 | | | |
| = SUM(A1:B3) | | | |
| = A3 ^ 2 | | | |

# Campus Life

To prepare for this assignment, complete the practice exercise: Formula Practice.

In this assignment you will create your own formulas, based on everyday events.

Start by downloading and opening the Campus Life workbook. ***Do not open the file directly from the internet.*** Save the file on your desktop first. Then open it.

**www.cob.sjsu.edu/BUS91L/Textbook/CampusLife.xls**

1. Enter your name and section number.

2. Enter data into the blank spaces in column B. You can make up your own data.

3. Create formulas and enter them in column C.

   a. Each formula should contain cell references.

   b. For example, in cell C43, type = B33. Do not enter a number.

   c. Only the formula in cell C13 should contain a number (0.0825 or 8.25%).

4. When you enter a formula in column C, you may see the formula in both the cell and in the formula bar above the worksheet. This is what I call "mirror" view. If you see a formula in the formula bar and the cell shows a zero, displays a number, or is blank, you are in what I call "flashcard" view.

   a. Switch between the two views by simultaneously pressing Ctrl + ~ on the keyboard.

   b. Check the math to be sure you understand what is being calculated.

5. With the worksheet in flashcard view, change some of the data to see what happens.

6. Return to mirror view. Click and drag to make the first 3 columns narrower.

7. Print the worksheet in mirror view.

   a. The Print settings should already be correct.

      i. The printer should be set to "Portrait" style.

      ii. Print the first three columns only, starting with row 4.

      iii. Select the printer setting "fit to one page."

8. Turn in the hard copy of the worksheet.*

**\*Your instructor may ask you to submit the assignment via email. Check the syllabus.**

# Copying Formulas

When you enter a formula into a cell you see the formula in the "formula bar" above the worksheet. If the formula also appears in the cell, you are in "mirror" view. If the formula does not appear in the cell, you are in "flashcard" view. Switch between the two views by simultaneously pressing Ctrl + ~ on the keyboard. Do this exercise in mirror view.

The goal of this exercise is to learn how cell references change when a formula is copied. Excel does this automatically. If you plan to copy a formula, and want to stop Excel from changing its cell reference, you add dollar signs to the cell reference. If one dollar sign is included in the formula, part of the cell reference won't change when the formula is copied into other cells. A cell reference with one dollar sign is called a Mixed Cell Reference. A cell reference with two dollar signs, called an Absolute Cell Reference, won't change at all when the formula is copied.

| Predict what will happen if the formula in Cell F6 is copied into: | | A different row? Try Cell F7 | A different column? Try Cell G6 | A different row and column? Try Cell G7 |
|---|---|---|---|---|
| = B2 | My Prediction | = B2 (Sample) | | |
| | What Excel Did | = B3 (Why?) | | |
| = B2 + C2 | My Prediction | | | |
| | What Excel Did | | | |
| = B2 + B3 | My Prediction | | | |
| | What Excel Did | | | |
| = $B2 + $B3 | My Prediction | | | |
| | What Excel Did | | | |
| = B$2 | My Prediction | | | |
| | What Excel Did | | | |
| = $B2 | My Prediction | | | |
| | What Excel Did | | | |
| = B$2 + C$2 | My Prediction | | | |
| | What Excel Did | | | |
| = $B$2 | My Prediction | | | |
| | What Excel Did | | | |

Enter the formula from the first row and column of the table into cell F6.

Predict how the cell references will change when the formula in cell F6 is copied into cells F7, G6, and G7. Record your predictions. Then copy the formula into cells F7, G6, and G7 and record the results. Compare your prediction to what Excel did.

Try to figure out the rules for how cell references change when formulas are copied.

Delete the contents of cells F6, F7, G6 and G7. Now try the next formula.

Continue until you have tested all 8 formulas.

# Creating a Times Table

Before starting this assignment, complete the copying formulas practice.

Open Excel.

1. Highlight cells A1 through D1 and merge them using the "merge and center" icon.

2. Type the words "Multiplication Table" into the merged cell. Format the text as bold and italicize it.

3. In Cells B2 through D2, enter the numbers from 2 through 4. Format them as bold. Center the numbers.

4. In Cells A3 to A21, enter the numbers from 2 through 20. Format them as bold. Center the numbers.

5. Enter formulas in rows 3 to 5, columns B to D, to calculate the value of 2 * 2, 2 * 3, 2 * 4, 3 * 2, 3 * 3, 3 * 4, 4 * 2, 4 * 3, and 4 * 4.

| Example | A | B | C | D |
|---|---|---|---|---|
| 1 | *Multiplication Table* | | | |
| 2 | | 2 | 3 | 4 |
| 3 | 2 | = 2 * 2 | = 2 * 3 | = 2 * 4 |
| 4 | 3 | = 3 * 2 | = 3 * 3 | = 3 * 4 |
| 5 | 4 | = 4 * 2 | = 4 * 3 | = 4 * 4 |
| 6 | 5 | | | |

6. When you enter the formula in cell B3, you may see the formula in both cell B3 and in the formula bar above the worksheet. This is what I call "mirror" view. If you see a formula in the formula bar and cell B3 shows 4, you are in what I call "flashcard" view. You can switch between the two views by simultaneously pressing Ctrl + ~ on the keyboard. To start this exercise, you should be in mirror view.

7. Switch to flashcard view. The result in cell B3 should be 4. Return to mirror view.

8. Edit the formulas to replace numbers with cell references. Cell B3 should say = A3 * B2

| Example | A | B | C | D |
|---|---|---|---|---|
| 1 | | *Multiplication Table* | | |
| 2 | | **2** | **3** | **4** |
| 3 | **2** | = A3 * B2 | = A3 * C2 | = A3 * D2 |
| 4 | **3** | = A4 * B2 | = A4 * C2 | = A4 * D2 |

9.  What are the two parts of the cell references which appear in every formula? Those are the parts that you don't want to change as you copy the formula into new rows and columns.

10. What are the two parts of the cell references in these formulas which change from row to row or column to column? Those are the parts that you want changing automatically as you copy the formula into new rows and columns.

11. Can you fix the formula in cell B3 so it will give the right results if you copy it into all of the cells in the Times Table? Some possible choices are

    = A$3 * $B2          = $A3 * $B2          = $A3 * B$2

    = A$3 * B$2          = A3 * $B$2          = $A$3 * B2

    *Note:* **Only <u>ONE</u> of these will work properly**

    *Hint: you always want to multiply by a specific column and by a specific row. You want that number and that row to stay unchanged when you copy the formula.*

12. Edit the formula in cell B3. (To edit a formula: Select the cell and then type in the formula bar or select the cell and click on the F2 function key.)

13. Copy the formula from B3 and paste it into the range B3:D21 (this is a rectangle with 19 rows and 3 columns) to complete the Multiplication Table.

14. Check your results in flashcard view. Do the formulas in the cells give the desired results?

15. Now look at the formulas in mirror view. What parts of the formulas changed when copied? What parts stayed the same? Why? Hold down the Ctrl + ~ keys to return to displaying the numbers.

| Desired Result | A | B | C | D |
|---|---|---|---|---|
| 1 | | *Multiplication Table* | | |
| 2 | | **2** | **3** | **4** |
| 3 | **2** | 4 | 6 | 8 |
| 4 | **3** | 6 | 9 | 12 |

16.  If the formulas don't fill in the table with your desired numbers, return to step 12 and experiment with a different combination of dollar signs. Repeats Steps 12, 13 and 14 until you get an accurate multiplication table. USE THE SAME FORMULA FOR EACH COLUMN AND ROW. DO NOT USE 3 FORMULAS!!

17.  When the formula produces the desired numbers, change the worksheet to mirror view.

18.  Print the worksheet in mirror view. *(Note: Formulas and numbers will be left-aligned. That's ok.)*

19.  Write your name and section number on the top of the printout and turn it in.

# CHAPTER 4

# Excel Formulas

A worksheet is a set of cells aligned in rows and columns. The cell content can be a statement containing a text message, a number, or a date. Dates are a special case. Although you see a date, the application stores the information as a number. It counts the days since Jan 1, 1900 and displays the result in date format. Because Excel stores each date as a number, you can add and subtract dates or easily put them in calendar order.

In Column A Row 1: (Cell A1) the content of A1 is a number with the value 3.
In Column B Row 1: (Cell B1) the content of B1 is a number with the value 5.
In Column A Row 2: (Cell A2) the content of A2 is a label "Text Message."
In Column B Row 2: (Cell B2) the content of B2 is a number, 37333, displayed as a date.

|        | Column A     | Column B       | Column C | Column D |
|--------|--------------|----------------|----------|----------|
| Row 1  | 3            | 5              |          |          |
| Row 2  | Text Message | March 18, 2002 |          |          |

The cell content can also be a formula. A formula asks a question and tells Excel to display the answer to that question. A formula always starts with an = sign. Think of a formula as "What is?" followed by a question. A cell containing a formula is like a flashcard; the cell displays the result of calculating the formula. The formula appears in the formula bar above the worksheet.

If you type a cell name in a formula, this is called a cell reference. The formula uses the value of the referenced cell to calculate its result. For example, if you type =A1 + 5 as a formula in cell C1, Excel will look into cell A1, then calculate the formula after converting the A1 cell reference into the value stored in A1. In this case the value is 3, and Excel will answer the question, what is 3 + 5? The answer is 8, which will be displayed in cell C1.

When you enter these statements or formulas in cell C1, here is what will be displayed:

| These statements in cell C1 | Display this in cell C1 | These formulas in cell C1 | Display this in cell C1 |
|---|---|---|---|
| 5+3 | 5+3 | =5+3 | 8 |
| B1+3 | B1+3 | =B1+3 | 8 |
| A1+B1 | A1+B1 | =A1+B1 | 8 |
| SUM(A1:B1) | SUM(A1:B1) | =SUM(A1:B1) | 8 |
| 5+B1 | 5+B1 | =5+B1 | 10 |

The =SUM(A1:B1) formula works by referencing a rectangle, called a range. A range's shape is described by the two cell addresses in opposite corners. For example, the range (A1:C2) would include the cells A1, B1, C1, A2, B2, and C2. The Sum instruction tells Excel to add the total of all the cells in the range. You can create Summation formulas automatically with an icon ($\Sigma$) found on the Standard toolbar. Summation is normally used to find the total of a row, column, or range of cells, not for simple addition of two cells. If you create a formula by clicking the Summation icon instead of the = sign, it wastes computer power and memory.

Example of ranges: B3:C4, E2:E4, C6:E7

| | A | B | C | D | E | F |
|---|---|---|---|---|---|---|
| 1 | | | | | | |
| 2 | | | | | | |
| 3 | | | | | | |
| 4 | | | | | | |
| 5 | | | | | | |
| 6 | | | | | | |
| 7 | | | | | | |
| 8 | | | | | | |

### Displaying Formulas

Sometimes you may want to display the actual formulas, instead of their results. You can highlight each individual cell and its formula will be displayed in the formula box located above the worksheet area. To view all of the cells as formulas, press Ctrl + ~ (tilde). The tilde key is in the upper left corner of the keyboard. Or, use the Tools menu under Options. There is a checkbox on the View tab where you can reset the worksheet to display formulas. You can also turn the gridlines on and off from this location.

## Copying Formulas

When a formula is copied, Excel automatically changes the row number in any cell references if the formula is copied into a different row. It automatically changes the column letters in any cell references if the formula is copied into a different column. The adjustment is equal to the number of rows or columns between the copied-into cell and the copied-from cell. In the examples given in the tables below, the formula in the source cell C4 was copied to cells E4 (increased column references by 2), C6 (increased row references by 2) and E6 (increased both row and column references by 2).

| | C | D | E | Comment |
|---|---|---|---|---|
| **4** | = A1+B2+C3 | | = C1+D2+E3 | Letters change when you copy a formula into a different column. Numbers change when you copy a formula into a different row. |
| **5** | | | | |
| **6** | = A3+B4+C5 | | = C3+D4+E5 | |

Cell references like those in the table above are called "relative (dynamic) cell references." You can add dollar signs to formulas to control the way Excel changes cell references when it copies a formula. Adding a dollar sign in a cell reference formula means: **Don't change the next part of this cell reference when copying this formula.** When a formula containing a dollar sign is copied to another cell, the part of the cell reference preceded by the $ will not change.

Cell references with dollar signs in front of just the number, or in front of just the letter, are called "Mixed Cell References." Use a mixed cell reference in a formula when you want to create a set of formulas that will *always* refer to either one **specific row:** A$1, or one **specific column:** $B2. If the formula should always use the same cell reference, add two dollar signs: $C$3. This is called an "Absolute Cell Reference."

You can combine absolute, mixed, and relative cell references in a single formula. The dollar sign does not change the resulting value of the formula in any way. For example, both = A1 + B2 and = $A$1 + $B$2 display exactly the same output.

In the following table, the formula in cell C4 was copied into other cells. Observe which row and column numbers changed and note the effect of the dollar signs.

| | C | D | E | Comment |
|---|---|---|---|---|
| **4** | = A$1+$B2 | | = C$1+$B2 | Notice that only the A and the 2 (in cell C4) change. Because of the $ symbol, the others don't change. |
| **5** | | | | |
| **6** | = A$1+$B4 | | = C$1+$B4 | |

One use for an absolute reference is to divide many numbers by the same constant. First set up a constant in a cell. Then enter a formula into another cell using an absolute cell reference in the formula. The formula can be copied and the reference to the cell containing the constant is unchanged. Changes to the cell containing the constant will cause the formulas that refer to this cell to recalculate their values.

### Some Common Error Messages

Error messages usually start with a Pound sign (#).

| | |
|---|---|
| ##### | If you see rail road tracks, your column is too narrow. Solution—widen the column. |
| #DIV/O! | You are dividing by an empty cell or zero. Solution—fix the formula's denominator. |
| #REF! | Your formula refers to a cell that no longer exists, due to a change in the worksheet. |
| #NAME? | Your formula contains text that Excel doesn't recognize. This could have many causes. Usually it's a typo or missing punctuation in a formula, like forgetting the = sign. |
| Circular | A formula can not reference the cell it is located in; this will generate an error message. You will see Circular followed by a cell reference in the area below the worksheet. |
| #N/A | You'll see this if a Lookup Table couldn't find a match to the text in the search input cell. |

### Formulas Using Multiple Worksheets

You can write formulas that refer to cells in other worksheets by including the worksheet name in the cell address. For example, if you typed =Sheet2!C4 in sheet 1, cell A3, that cell would display the contents of cell C4 in sheet 2. If the contents of sheet 2 cell C4 was a formula, you would see the results of the formula, not a formula.

### Order of Operations

If a formula contains multiple calculations, Excel calculates the parts of the formula in this order: calculations in parentheses, then percentages, then exponentiation, then multiplication and division, then addition and subtraction, always moving from left to right. Use parentheses to force Excel to do the calculations in the order you want. For example = 3+4*2 will display 11, since Excel would do the multiplication first, while = (3+4)*2 will display 14.

### Some Examples of Commonly Used Formulas are Given Below

There is no one right way to write a formula; getting the correct result is what matters. Spaces are not necessary in the formulas, but they are included below to allow for ease of understanding.

**This Table is used with the Sample Formulas below:**

| | A | B | C | D |
|---|---|---|---|---|
| 1 | 25 | 28 | 95 | |
| 2 | 42 | 91 | 14 | |
| 3 | 3 | 4 | 5 | |

## SAMPLE FORMULAS:

| Type of Equation: | Entered in Cell D3: | Result Displayed in D3: |
|---|---|---|
| Addition of Two Cells | = A2 + B3 | 46 |
| Addition of a Constant | = B1 + 25 | 53 |
| Addition of a Row of Cells | = SUM (A1:C1) | 148 |
| Addition of a Column of Cells | = SUM (B1:B3) | 123 |
| Addition of a Range of Cells | = SUM (B1:C3) | 237 |
| Addition of Scattered Cells | = SUM (A2,B1,C3) | 75 |
| Subtraction of a Constant | = C1 – 10 | 85 |
| Subtraction of a Cell | = B2 – B1 | 63 |
| Multiplication by a Constant | = A3 * 20 | 60 |
| Multiplication of Two Cells | = B3 * C3 | 20 |
| Multiplication by a % | = A1 * .40 | 10 |
| Multiplication by a % | = B1 * 25% | 7 |
| Division by a Constant | = C1 / 5 | 19 |
| Division by a Cell | = A2 / C2 | 3 |
| Exponentiation (Squaring) | = B3 ^ 2 | 16 |
| Exponentiation (Cubing) | = A3 ^ 3 | 27 |
| Square Roots | = SQRT(A1) | 5 |
| Square Roots | = A1 ^ 0.5 | 5 |
| Cube Roots | = B1 ^ (1/3) | 3.036589 |
| Increasing by a Percentage (4%) | = A1 + (A1 * .04) | 26 |
| Increasing by a Percentage (4%) | = A1 * 1.04 | 26 |
| Increasing by a Percentage (4%) | = A1 + (A1 * 4%) | 26 |
| Decreasing by a Percentage (8%) | = A1 - (A1 *.08) | 23 |
| Decreasing by a Percentage (8%) | = A1 *.92 | 23 |
| Decreasing by a Percentage (8%) | = A1 – (A1 * 8%) | 23 |
| Calculate a Percentage (Each Part/Sum) | =A3 / $D$3 | 25% (Format as a %) |
| Average of a Column | = AVG (B1:B3) | 41 |
| Average of a Row | = AVG (A3:C3) | 4 |
| Average of a Range | = AVG (B1:C2) | 57 |

| SPECIAL CASES: | | |
|---|---|---|
| Formula referring to a cell in another worksheet | = Sheet2!C4 | The contents of cell C4 in Sheet 2. Excel displays the results of the formula. |
| Mixed Cell Reference for a row: | = A$1+3 | The row number stays unchanged when the formula is copied. |
| Mixed Cell Reference for a column: | = $A2+3 | The column letter stays unchanged when the formula is copied. |
| Absolute Cell Reference | = 78 / $A$3 | The row number and column letter are unchanged if the formula is copied. |

# Payroll Forecast

From the Tools menu, Customize submenu, Options tab, select all options except "large icons."

Prepare a staffing guide to estimate weekly payroll expense for a coffee shop.

- The coffee shop is open 96 hours per week, Monday - Saturday, 6am to 10pm.
- The manager works 48 hours per week at $20 per hour w/o O/T.
- Assume benefit costs are 30% of gross wages.
- Minimum wage is $6.75 Add more rows with job titles. Estimate the pay rates.
- Hours per Week means the total hours worked by all employees in that classification.
- Use formulas to calculate the totals for columns D, E, F, and G.
- The formula for "As a % of All Payroll" = Total Cost in each row / the sum of the Total Costs column (shaded in gray).

Sample:

| Job Title | Pay Rate | Hours per Week | Gross Wages | Benefits | Total Cost | As a % of All Payroll |
|---|---|---|---|---|---|---|
| Manager | $20.00 | =1*8*6 | $ 960 | $288 | $1248 | % |
| Wait-staff | $ 6.75 | =2*16*6 | $1296 | $389 | $1685 | % |
| Cashiers | $ | | $ | $ | $ | % |
| Diswashers | $ | | $ | $ | $ | % |
| Other job titles | $ | | $ | $ | $ | % |
| Totals | $ | | $ | $ | $ | 100% |

Hours per week = The number of employees working at the same time, multiplied by the number of hours per day that position will be staffed, multiplied by the number of days per week.

| | |
|---|---|
| Is there a shortcut to calculate the totals? | Hint – use the AutoSum icon. |
| Is there a shortcut to calculate the % of payroll? | Hint – use dollar signs in the formula. |
| Are there any shortcuts to format the numbers? | Hints – use the format paintbrush. Use the increase / decrease decimals icons. Use the % and $ icons. |

Our financial backer didn't like our table. We will find ways to improve it.

- Our benefit cost was assumed to be 30%. How can we improve that estimate? In the rows below the table, list all of the benefits: Social Security, Medicare, Health Care Insurance Plan, State Disability Insurance, Workers Comp, Vacation Pay, Retirement Benefits, Sick Pay, Holiday Pay. Beside each, show the cost as a % of wages.

- Create a Total Benefits line and find the sum of the percents.

- Fix the Benefits formula in column E: Replace the 30% with a reference to the cell which shows the Total of the Benefits percentages. Use $ signs in the cell reference.

- Calculate your payroll cost for 6 months. (Multiply total cost by 26 weeks.)

How does the payroll cost for 6 months compare to your estimated revenues of $350,000? Are you making a profit? Do you need to change any assumptions?

- Change a few assumptions. See how the worksheet is affected.

- Add a worksheet title. [Insert a new row A. Merge Cells. Enter a title for the table.]

- Add colors and cell borders. [toolbar icons]

# Sales Forecast

For this assignment, you will create a Coffee Shop Sales Forecast for a six month period.

Before you begin creating a worksheet, it is a good idea to create a drawing or rough outline of how you want it to look. Refer to this sample. My numbers are rounded so they won't exactly match yours.

| | A | B | C | D | E | F | G | H | I |
|---|---|---|---|---|---|---|---|---|---|
| 1 | Business Productivity Tools | Java Juice Sales Forecast | | | | | | | |
| 2 | Prepared by: Your Name | | | | | | | | |
| 3 | | Jan-00 | Feb-00 | Mar-00 | Apr-00 | May-00 | Jun-00 | Total | % |
| 4 | Food Sales | | | | | | | | |
| 5 | Sandwiches | $17,500 | $18,000 | $18,500 | $19,000 | $19,500 | $20,000 | $112,500 | 48.1% |
| 6 | Soup/Salads | 8,000 | 8,720 | 9,505 | 10,360 | 11,293 | 12,309 | 60,187 | 25.7% |
| 7 | Desserts | 9,000 | 9,450 | 9,923 | 10,419 | 10,940 | 11,487 | 61,219 | 26.2% |
| 8 | Total Food Sales | $34,500 | $36,170 | $37,928 | $39,779 | $41,733 | $43,796 | $233,906 | 100% |
| 9 | | | | | | | | | |
| 10 | Beverage Sales | | | | | | | | |
| 11 | Coffee | $14,000 | $14,420 | $14,853 | $15,298 | $15,757 | $16,229 | $90,557 | 46.7% |
| 12 | Tea | 6,120 | 6,120 | 6,120 | 6,120 | 6,120 | 6,120 | 36,720 | 18.9% |
| 13 | Beer/Wine | 5,200 | 5,044 | 4,893 | 4,746 | 4,604 | 4,465 | 28,952 | 14.9% |
| 14 | Juice | 1,950 | 2,243 | 2,579 | 2,966 | 3,411 | 3,922 | 17,071 | 8.8% |
| 15 | Soft Drinks | 3,250 | 3,330 | 3,410 | 3,490 | 3,570 | 3,650 | 20,700 | 10.7% |
| 16 | Total Beverage Sales | $30,520 | $31,157 | $31,855 | $32,620 | $33,462 | $34,386 | $194,000 | 100% |
| 17 | | | | | | | | | |
| 18 | Ingredient Costs | | | | | | | | |
| 19 | Food Costs | $7,590 | $7,957 | $8,344 | $8,751 | $9,181 | $9,635 | $51,459 | |
| 20 | Beverage Costs | $3,357 | $3,427 | $3,504 | $3,588 | $3,681 | $3,783 | $21,340 | |
| 21 | | | | | | | | | |
| 22 | Net Revenue | $54,073 | $55,942 | $57,935 | $60,059 | $62,332 | $64,765 | $355,106 | |
| 23 | | | | | | | | | |
| 24 | Ratios | | | | | | | | |
| 25 | Food Cost as a % of Sales | 22% | | | | | | | |
| 26 | Beverage Cost as a % of Sales | 11% | | | | | | | Sample |

## Directions

1. Type "Java Juice Sales Forecast", into cell B1. Format the heading as bold and use a size 16 font. Use the Merge and Center icon to merge cells B1 to I1 (Eye One).

2. Enter dates in cells B3 to G3: "Jan-00" to "Jun-00." (Hint: don't type in the words, use number keys: 1-1-2000 or 1/1/2000.) Format the cells to show the Month and Year as shown in the sample. (Hint: use the Numbers tab in the Format dialog box). In cell H3 type the word Total. In I3 type the % sign. Format cells B3 to I3 as centered, bold, with a red font.

3. Add Text to cells A1 to A26, as shown in the sample. Include your name and section number in cell A2.

4. For the Food Sales, Beverage Sales, Ingredient Costs, and Ratios cells, use a blue font and apply an underline format.

5. For the Sandwich, Soups/Salads, Desserts, Coffee, Tea, Beer/Wine, Juices, and Soft Drinks cells use a green font.

6. For the three food categories and the five beverage categories, enter sales values for January in column B. You can either use the numbers provided in the sample or make up your own. When you enter these numbers try to be realistic. Remember that our coffee shop is open 6 days a week, 16 hours a day, which equals about 420 hours per month.

7. Create formulas to obtain the sales values for February. Enter these formulas in Column C.
   a. Row 5: Sales of Sandwiches will increase by $500 each month.
   b. Row 6: Sales of Soups/Salads will increase 9% each month.
   c. Row 7: Sales of Desserts will increase 5% each month.
   d. Row 11: Sales of Coffee will increase by 3% each month.
   e. Row 12: Sales of Tea will not change. Use a formula, not a number.
   f. Row 13: Sales of Beer/Wine will decrease by 3% each month.
   g. Row 14: Sales of Juices will increase by 15% each month.
   h. Row 15: Sales of Soft Drinks will increase by $80 each month.

8. Format the cells in row 5 and row 11 as Currency with no decimal places. (Hint: the currency icon on the toolbar is mislabeled. It is actually accounting format. You will have to use the Number tab in the format dialog box to find the currency format.)

9. Format the cells in the other sales categories as "General" numbers with no decimal places.

10. Use the summation icon 'Σ' to enter formulas in cells B8, C8, B16 and C16. The formulas will refer to the set of numbers directly above these cells. Format the cells as currency with no decimal places.

11. Format the cells B25 and B26, as percentages with no decimal places.

12. Enter a number between 20% and 30% in cell B25. (Food Ingredient Cost Ratio)

13. Enter a number between 10% and 20% in cell B26. (Beverage Ingredient Cost Ratio)

14. Enter a *formula* for "Food Costs" in cell B19. (Hint: =Total Food Sales * the Food Cost Ratio in cell B25.) Use an absolute cell reference referring to cell B25 for the Food Cost Ratio. Format cell B19 as currency with no decimal places. Copy the formula to cell C19. Check to make sure the cell reference still refers to cell B25. (Hint: Use dollar signs in your formula.)

15. Enter a *formula* for "Beverage Costs" in cell B20. (Hint: =Total Beverage Sales * the Beverage Cost Ratio.) Use an absolute cell reference referring to cell B26 for the Beverage Cost Ratio. Format cell B20 as currency with no decimal places. Copy the formula to cell C20. Check to make sure the cell reference still refers to cell B26. (Hint: Use dollar signs in your formula.)

16. Enter a formula in cell B22 to calculate the Net Revenue. This will include Food Sales + Beverage Sales - Food Cost - Beverage Cost. Format it as Currency, with no decimal places. Copy the formula into cell C22.

17. You should now have finished entering formulas in Column C, rows 5 through 22. Copy the formulas into columns D through G.

18. Using the summation icon 'Σ', insert =SUM formulas into column H showing the total for each row (5 through 22) that contains data.

19. Format the cells in column I (EYE) as percents and add a light yellow background.

20. In cell I5 write a formula, using cell references, to show the sandwich sales as a percentage of total food sales. (Hint: Divide Total Sandwich Sales by Total Food Sales.) Include 2 dollar signs in the divisor cell reference. Copy the formula in cell I5 into cells I6, and I7. Change the number of decimal places to 1.

21. In cell I11 write a formula, using cell references, to show the coffee sales as a percentage of total beverage sales. (Hint: Divide Total Coffee Sales by Total Beverage Sales.) Include two dollar signs in the divisor cell reference. Copy the formula in cell I11 into cells I12, I13, I14, and I15.

22. Insert =SUM formulas into cells I8 and I16 to show the total of the percentages. Format the cells to show no decimal places.

    You can use the data validation feature to provide messages to guide spreadsheet users.

23. Click on cell A3. On the Menu Bar, select Data, then Validation. Click on the Input Message tab. In the title box, type: "Warning!" In the input message box, type: "Leave this cell blank." Click OK.

    Did your message appear? Click on another cell. Did the message go away? Click back on A3.

24. Add lines (hint: use the borders icon) to your Forecast as shown on the sample.

25. Turn the gridlines off. This option is found on the Tools menu, Options submenu, View tab.

26. Select the entire worksheet and increase the height of the rows to 14. (Hint: From the Menu Bar, select Format, Row, Height and enter 14 and click OK.) Click on cell A1. Click and drag to reduce the height of rows 9, 17 and 21 to 9.00. Increase the height of row 1 to 21.00.

27. Change the name of the worksheet tab to Sales. (Hint: right-click on the tab.)

28. Create a copy of the Sales spreadsheet. (Hint: right-click on the tab.) Rename the tab on the copy to Formulas. In the Formulas worksheet, switch to the view that shows the formulas in the cells. (Ctrl + ~.)

29. Print both the Sales worksheet and the Formulas worksheet. (Hint: use the landscape setting instead of portrait.)

30. Save the file.

# CHAPTER 5

# The *ABC!* Method to Creating Charts

## Accentuate the Labels and Data. *Build* the Chart. *Change* its Appearance.

### Accentuate the Labels and Data

You can use the mouse to highlight (Accentuate) the cells in the worksheet that include the information needed to build a chart. The selected rows or columns (including the labels) must contain the same number of cells.

The first step is always to accentuate the row or column of labels for the fields of data. If your data will have a name for each row, called a Series Name, your row of labels should start with a blank cell. Highlight that blank cell when you highlight the row.

Next, highlight your data (numbers). If the rows or columns are not next to one another, hold down the Control key while highlighting different rows.

Each row of data usually starts with a Series Name for the data row. If your data has series names, select these cells when you accentuate the data.

For example: highlight cells C3 to I3 for the labels, hold down Control, highlight cells C6 to I9 for four rows of data, keep holding down Control, and highlight cells: C12 to I12 for a fifth row of data.

Be sure to highlight the labels first. The labels row (or column) must start with a blank cell if you want to include a series name for the rows of data. If your finger slips and you don't completely highlight all the desired cells in a row or column, start over.

### Build the Chart

Click the Chart Wizard icon on the Standard toolbar. The wizard builds the chart. The chart wizard is limited in what it can do, so you will change the appearance of your chart after you build it. For example, the wizard only allows a single line of text for the chart title, but you can change this after the chart is built. You can move both forward and backward through the wizard.

1. Choose one of the available **chart types.**

2. Look at a preview of the charts and select one. Move to the next dialog box.

3. Confirm that your data is correct. Move to the next dialog box.

4. Move from tab to tab, left to right, as you move through the third dialog box. Enter the title. Specify additional **options.** Look at every tab to be sure you have not missed any crucial options. Move to the fourth dialog box.

5.  Choose whether the chart is to be created as an **embedded chart** (an object) within a specific worksheet, or whether it is to be created in its own **chart sheet.**

### Change its Appearance

**To change the appearance of any object in the chart:** Right-click on it. Choose format. You can change the font, size, color, and style of existing text anywhere in the chart. Graphics can be re-colored and re-sized. You can add shadows to chart elements. Also notice that a Chart option appears in the menu bar when a chart is selected.

**To work with individual data points:** (For Example - Pie Wedges) Left click on the data series. All points are selected. Click again on the individual data point. The single point is selected. Left click to drag, right click to format.

**To edit the title:** Click twice on it. You can insert extra lines (the wizard allows just 1).

**To move or resize the legend:** Click and drag.

**To name the chart sheet:** Rename the tab by right-clicking on it.

**To move the chart:** You can resize, move, copy, or delete a chart or any of the objects within the chart. If you resize the chart you may need to resize the fonts inside the chart.

**To change the chart after it has been created:** You can return to any dialog box in the wizard. Right click in the chart background. Choose from the four "wizard" options. Or use the chart menu.

**To remove a set of data points:** Right click within an element of the series. Select clear.

**To refresh the chart's data:** A chart is linked to the worksheet on which it is based. If you change any of the worksheet's data, the chart automatically adjusts to the new data.

**To add additional rows of data to the chart:**

- **Mouse method:** Highlight a row of data. Left click again and move the cursor to get an arrow. Click and drag the arrow into the chart area. Release the mouse.

- **Wizard method:** From the Source Data, Series tab, click on Add Row. Click the icon in the name box. Use the mouse to highlight the worksheet cell containing the name of your data. Press Enter. Click the icon in the Values box. Highlight the cells with the data and press Enter. Click OK.

**To add colorful background effects:** Right click on any graphic element of the chart. Select format. Click on "Fill Effects." If you are formatting a graphic from the Drawing toolbar, you may have to use the "Color" pull-down box to find the "Fill Effects" button.

**To combine graphics with a chart:** Use the Drawing toolbar to add text boxes, arrows and lines. Adding clip art, WordArt and pictures can make a plain chart look spectacular.

**To attach the graphics to your chart:** Select the objects by holding down the Control key and left clicking on the chart and on the graphics. Right click and select group.

EXERCISE **1**

# Bar Chart

From the Tools menu, Customize submenu, Options tab, select all options except "large icons." We will build a bar chart showing monthly food sales, by category, for 6 months.

Data used for the charts can be found at *www.cob.sjsu.edu/BUS91L/Textbook/chartdata.xls.*

**Do not open the file from the web.** Save the file on your desktop first, and then open it.

For sample pictures of the charts go to *www.cob.sjsu.edu/BUS91L/Textbook/Ch5pics1.htm.*

|   | A | B | C | D | E | F | G |
|---|---|---|---|---|---|---|---|
| 3 |   | **Jan-00** | **Feb-00** | **Mar-00** | **Apr-00** | **May-00** | **Jun-00** |
| 4 | **Food Sales** |   |   |   |   |   |   |
| 5 | **Sandwiches** | $17,500 | $18,000 | $18,500 | $19,000 | $19,500 | $20,000 |
| 6 | **Soups/Salads** | 8,000 | 8,720 | 9,505 | 10,360 | 11,293 | 12,309 |
| 7 | **Desserts** | 9,000 | 9,450 | 9,923 | 10,419 | 10,940 | 11,487 |
| 8 | **Total Food Sales** | $34,500 | $36,170 | $37,928 | $39,779 | $41,733 | $43,796 |

1. Accent (highlight with the mouse) the labels in cells A3 to G3. Cells in Row 3 contain your X Axis Labels. Highlight them first. Include the blank cell in A3.

2. Cells in Rows 5, 6, and 7 contain data. Hold down Control. This will keep the cells in Row 3 highlighted. Use the mouse to highlight the rows of data. Cells A5, A6, and A7 contain the "series names" for the rows of data. Include these cells with the data.

3. Build the chart – click the Chart Wizard icon.

4. Select the Chart Type: Stacked Bar.

5. The chart's title is Food Sales, with the axes labeled as Months and Revenues.

6. Place the chart in a new sheet. Call the sheet "FoodSales." (Don't include any spaces.)

7. Click twice in the title. Add your name and section number on a second line.

8. Format all of the text elements as 12-point font.

9. Format the Revenues axis so that the numbers are aligned to 45 degrees.

10. Format the Revenues axis scale: maximum value is $45,000 and the minimum is $0. The Auto option next to maximum and minimum should be unchecked.

11. Add light green shading and a shadow to the legend.

12. Drag the legend to align its bottom line with the chart's bottom line. Make the box taller.

13. Fill the Sandwiches set of data points with a Bouquet texture. Add a shadow.

14. Fill the Soups/Salads data points with Pink Tissue Paper texture. Add a shadow.

15. Fill the Desserts set of data points with a Stationery texture. Add a shadow.

16. Fill in the plot area background using the preset gradient Daybreak.

17. Fill the chart's background with an 80% pattern. Use a light yellow foreground.

18. Add graphic elements from the drawing toolbar (WordArt, Clip Art, Shape, Call Out, Etc.).

Alter some data. Notice how the chart changes.

*EXERCISE*

# Building Charts

This project will use data from: *www.cob.sjsu.edu/BUS91L/Textbook/ChartData.xls* to create four charts. First save the ChartData file to the desktop and then open it.

For sample pictures of the charts go to *www.cob.sjsu.edu/BUS91L/Textbook/Ch5pics2.htm.*

Remember the ABC's: Accentuate the labels and data, Build the chart, and then Change its appearance. Labels include the field names (i.e. months) and the series names (column A in the data rows). Accentuate the months' row first and include the blank cell in column A. By including the blank cell, you will be able to include the series names found in column A when you select your data rows.

Chart One: A Column Chart showing monthly juice sales for each of the 6 months.
Chart type: Stacked Column with 3-D Visual Effect.

1. The chart should have a title (Juice Sales), with the X and Z axes labeled as "Months" and "Sales." Don't label the Y axis.
2. Place the chart in a chart sheet, with the sheet tab labeled ChartA.
3. Add your name and section number on a second line in the title.
4. Format all of the text and numbers in the chart using a 12-point font size.
5. Fill in the walls area background using a 1-color gradient.
6. Fill in the floor area with a texture.
7. Fill the columns of your graph with a pattern.
8. Add light yellow shading and a shadow to the legend.
9. Click and drag to enlarge the legend box and then move it to the lower left of the chart.
10. Add a texture to the chart area background.
11. Add a graphic element from the drawing toolbar (WordArt, Clip Art, Shape, Call Out, Etc.). You do not have to use the same clip art as the ones shown in the samples.

Chart Two: Line Graph with 3 lines: Total Food Sales, Total Beverage Sales, and Net Revenue, by month.
Chart type: Line with markers (not stacked).

1. The chart should have a title: "Sales and Profits."
2. Label the axes as "Months" and "Sales Forecast."
3. The chart should have a legend at the top, as shown in the sample.
4. The chart should contain major horizontal gridlines.

5. Place the chart in a chart sheet with the sheet tab labeled ChartB.

6. Format all of the text and numbers in the chart using a 12-point font size.

7. Change the color of the Net Sales line to blue. Increase its weight by one level.

8. Add a shadow to the Net Sales marker and increase its size to 11 points. Give it a blue foreground and a white background. Change the marker to a square.

9. Change the color of the Beverage line to red. Increase its weight by one level.

10. Add a shadow to the Beverage marker and increase its size to 11 points. Give it a red foreground and background. Change the marker to a circle.

11. Change the color of the Food line to green. Increase its weight by one level.

12. Increase the size of the Food marker to 13 points. Give it a black foreground and a yellow background. Change the marker to a triangle.

13. Fill in the plot area background with a gold preset gradient angled diagonally up.

14. Add a label to each line, using text boxes. Use a bold, 14-point font.

Chart Three: Pie Chart showing Food Ingredient Costs by month. Chart type: Pie with a 3-D visual effect.

1. The chart should have a title: "Food Costs."

2. Do not show the legend.

3. Label the pie wedges with both category and percentage. Use a "new line" separator.

4. Place the chart in a chart sheet with the sheet tab labeled ChartC.

5. Add your name and section number on the second line of the title.

6. Format all of the text and numbers in the chart using a bold, italics, 12-point font.

7. Format the percentages to show 2 decimal places.

8. Drag the June wedge away from the rest of the pie. (Hint: this requires three left clicks on the wedge. Drag it after the third click.)

9. Change the color of the wedges to different varieties of blue.

10. Fill the chart area background with a texture.

11. Add a graphic element from the drawing toolbar (WordArt, Clip Art, Shape, Call Out, Etc.). You do not have to use the same clip art as the ones shown in the samples.

Chart Four: Column Chart showing monthly Beverage Sales by type. Include all five rows of data.
Chart type: Stacked Column.

1. The chart should have a title: "Monthly Beverage Sales."

2. Label the x-axis as "Months" and the y-axis as "Sales."

3. Keep the legend on the right.

4. Build the chart in your sales data worksheet, ***not on a separate chart/worksheet.***

5. Drag the chart down the page so it is not covering the worksheet data.

6. Change all of the font sizes to 12-point and make them all bold. Hint, you can click in the chart background to change the format of all of the fonts.

7. Fill in the plot area background with a texture.

8. Fill in the sections of the columns using a 1-color "from center" gradient.

9. Add a color and a shadow to the legend.

10. Fill in the chart area background with a 1-color gradient.

11. Add a shadow and rounded corners to the chart. Note: the rounded corners option is only available in worksheets, not in chart sheets.

12. Add a graphic element from the drawing toolbar (WordArt, Clip Art, Shape, Call Out, Etc.). You do not have to use the same clip art as the ones shown in the samples.

13. Be sure to put the sheet tabs in order. (Sales, ChartA, ChartB, ChartC.)

## How to Make Corrections

1. If you need to make a correction to the chart type, change the data source, or change the chart options, right-click on the background of the chart, or use the Chart menu, to reenter the chart wizard.

2. For example, if you didn't highlight the cells in column A when you highlighted your labels and data, the legends in the charts will say series 1, series 2, etc. You can fix this later by going back into the wizard.

   - Right click on the chart background. Choose Source Data. A dialog box opens. Choose the Series Tab. To the right of the box that shows series 1, series 2, etc., you'll see an empty box next to the word Name.

   - Click on series 1. Click in the Name box. Now Click on the tab of the worksheet that contains your data. Find the cell with the name that matches the row of data and click on it.

   - Go back to the wizard dialog box. Click on Series 2. Click in the Name box. Now Click on the tab of the worksheet that contains your data. Find the cell with the name that matches the row of data and click on it. Keep going until you have given each series a name.

# CHAPTER 6

# Excel Forms and Functions

## Functions

### Advanced Formulas

Excel has a built-in set of advanced formulas and functions. To access them, click on the fx symbol to the left of the formula bar, or click on the pull down box next to the AutoSum Icon, or use the Insert menu. Here are some commonly used functions:

| | |
|---|---|
| **SUM** | **Example = SUM(C3:G9)** |
| | Result: Total of all numbers in the range. |
| **AVERAGE** | **Example = AVERAGE(C3:G9)** |
| | Result: Average of all numbers in the range. |
| **COUNTIF** | **Example = COUNTIF(C3:G9, ">55")** |
| | Result: # of cells in the range containing numbers greater than 55. |
| | Used in counting groups of similar numbers within a set of data. |
| **TODAY()** | **Example = TODAY()** |
| | Result = current date. Useful for forms that require a date. |
| **ROUND** | **Example = ROUND(A4/3,2)** |
| | Result if A4 = 5 then 5/3 = 1.6666 which is rounded to 1.67. |
| **IF** | **Example = IF(A4<4, "Small number", 40)** |
| | The cell containing this function will display either Small Number, or 40, depending on the contents of cell A4. |
| **VLOOKUP** | **Example = VLookUp(C4,G3:K12,3)** |
| | The cell containing this function will display the number in the third column of the range G3 to K12, if the contents of cell C4 match an entry in one of the cells in the first column of the range. |

### IF Functions

We can use an IF Function to select what appears in a cell, choosing between two different options. Which option is displayed in the cell containing the IF function depends on the result of an equation. If the conditions in the equation are met, the first option is displayed. If not, the second option is displayed.

An IF function has 3 parts. The first part is an equation comparing a constant and a variable. The second and third parts show the two options for Excel to display. The variable in the equation is always entered into a different cell from the cell containing the IF function.

**EXAMPLE: = IF (A4 > 4, A4 + 2, 3)** Cell A4 contains the variable, the number 4 is the constant. If our test condition is met, (i.e. A4 > 4), Excel selects the first formula. The cell containing the IF function will display the sum of the value in cell A4 and 2. Otherwise, the cell containing the IF function will show the number 3.

If cell C4 contains the IF function, here's what would happen as the value in cell A4 is changed:

- If cell A4 contains a 6, Excel displays 8, (the contents of cell A4 [6] + 2 ) in cell C4.
- If cell A4 contains a 2, Excel displays the number 3 in cell C4.
- If cell A4 contains a 4, Excel displays the number 3 in cell C4.

IF functions also work with strings (text and/or numbers in quotes): =IF (A4>74%, "Pass," "Fail"). In this example, if we put the IF function in cell C4, then cell C4 would display either Pass or Fail, depending on the value in cell A4.

# Multiple Worksheet Practice

Create a form to track souvenir sales, edit it for each quarter, and create a mid-year summary.

Items sold = [Starting Inventory + Purchases – Ending Inventory.] Use an IF function to decide when to order more inventory. [IF (Starting Inv <100, order 144 more, if not, order zero more)]

## Build the Generic Form

1. Rename the worksheets as Q1, Q2, and Summary.

2. Select all tabs. (Right click on any tab. Select All. The tabs all turn white.)

3. Create the form as shown below. It will automatically be copied into all of the worksheets.

| | A | B | C | D | E | F |
|---|---|---|---|---|---|---|
| **1** | | | | **Souvenir Sales** | | |
| **2** | | | | | | |
| **3** | **Item** | **Units** | **Starting Inv** | **Purchases** | **Ending Inv** | **Items Sold** |
| **4** | **Mugs** | **Each** | | =IF(C4<100,144,0) | | =C4+D4–E4 |
| **5** | **Shirts** | **Each** | | =IF(C5<100,144,0) | | =C5+D5–E5 |
| **6** | **Posters** | **Each** | | =IF(C6<100,144,0) | | =C6+D6–E6 |
| **7** | **CD's** | **Each** | | =IF(C7<100,144,0) | | =C7+D7–E7 |
| **8** | **Caps** | **Each** | | =IF(C8<100,144,0) | | =C8+D8–E8 |

## Complete the First Quarter (Q1) Worksheet

1. Deselect all tabs. (Click on a tab that is not showing in bold type.) Click on the Q1 tab.

2. Type "Quarter 1" in cell A2.

3. In column C, enter the Starting Inv values, as given below.

4. In column E, enter the Ending Inv numbers, as given below.

5. The If Functions in column D should tell you to order Posters and Caps, but nothing else.

| | A | B | C | D | E | F |
|---|---|---|---|---|---|---|
| **1** | | | | Souvenir Sales | | |
| **2** | | | | Quarter 1 | | |
| **3** | **Item** | **Units** | **Starting Inv** | **Purchases** | **Ending Inv** | **Items Sold** |
| **4** | **Mugs** | **Each** | 260 | =IF(C4<100,144,0) | 52 | =C4+D4–E4 |
| **5** | **Shirts** | **Each** | 160 | =IF(C5<100,144,0) | 104 | =C5+D5–E5 |
| **6** | **Posters** | **Each** | 80 | =IF(C6<100,144,0) | 64 | =C6+D6–E6 |
| **7** | **CD's** | **Each** | 100 | =IF(C7<100,144,0) | 96 | =C7+D7–E7 |
| **8** | **Caps** | **Each** | 60 | =IF(C8<100,144,0) | 132 | =C8+D8–E8 |

To write formulas that refer to cells in other worksheets, include the name of the other worksheet, followed by an exclamation mark, in your cell reference.

For example: =Q2!E4 refers to cell E4 in the Q2 worksheet.

### Complete the Second Quarter (Q2) Worksheet

1. Type "Quarter 2" in cell A2.
2. The Starting Inv for each quarter = the Ending Inv from the previous quarter. The formula for the Starting Inv for Q2 Mugs is the Ending Inv for Q1 Mugs: =Q1!E4.
3. In column C, enter formulas for the Starting Inv for each product.
4. In column E, enter a formula = to 1/4 * the (Starting Inv + Purchases) for each item.

### Complete the Summary Worksheet

1. Change the subtitle in row 2 to Mid-Year Summary - followed by your name.
2. The Starting Inv on the Mid-Year Summary = the first quarter's Starting Inv.
3. The Ending Inv on the Mid-Year Summary = the second quarter's Ending Inv.
4. Delete the formulas in the Purchases column.
5. Enter new formulas in the purchases column, equal to the sum of Purchases from the two quarters. For example, Mug Purchases =Q1!D4+Q2!D4.
6. You can point and click to build this formula. Start with an = sign in cell D4 in the Summary worksheet. Click on cell D4 in the Q1 worksheet. Type +. Click on cell D4 in the Q2 worksheet. Press Enter.
7. Copy the formula from D4 into rows 5–8.

| | A | B | C | D | E | F |
|---|---|---|---|---|---|---|
| 1 | Souvenir Sales | | | | | |
| 2 | Mid-Year Summary—My Name | | | | | |
| 3 | Item | Units | Starting Inv | Purchases | Ending Inv | Items Sold |
| 4 | Mugs | Each | =Q1!C4 | | =Q2!E4 | =C4+D4–E4 |
| 5 | Shirts | Each | =Q1!C5 | | =Q2!E5 | =C5+D5–E5 |
| 6 | Posters | Each | =Q1!C6 | | =Q2!E6 | =C6+D6–E6 |
| 7 | CD's | Each | =Q1!C7 | | =Q2!E7 | =C7+D7–E7 |
| 8 | Caps | Each | =Q1!C8 | | =Q2!E8 | =C8+D8–E8 |

### Your manager asks for more information on the Mid-Year Summary Worksheet

1. Add a column showing Price.
2. Make up a sales price for each item and enter it in the column.
3. Add a column showing Unit Cost.
4. Make up a cost for each item and enter it in the column.
5. Add a column showing Revenue [= Items Sold * Price].
6. Add a column showing Total Cost [= Items Sold * Unit Cost].
7. Add a column showing Profit [= Revenue – Total Cost].
8. Format columns G–K as centered, Currency Style, with no decimal places.

**Sample:** *www.cob.sjsu.edu/bus91L/textbook/ch6pics.htm*

— comment: Insert / comment

# Delivery Form

From the Tools menu, Customize submenu, Options tab, select all options except "large icons."

This assignment will introduce sorting and managing data using If Functions, lists, and VLookUp tables. You'll integrate Excel with the web, work with multiple spreadsheets, and learn more about formatting.

Data used: *www.cob.sjsu.edu/BUS91L/Textbook/DeliveryForm.xls*

***Do not open the file from the web.*** Save the file on your desktop. Then open the file.

## Background

When you want a formula to refer to a cell (or range) in another worksheet, put the worksheet name followed by an ! sign in your formula before the cell address.

For example, =Lists!A5 refers to cell A5 in the Lists worksheet.

An IF Formula has three parts. Part one is an equation comparing two values; one value is a constant and one is a variable. Part two is the result to display if the conditions in the equation are met. Part three is what to display if the conditions in the equation are not met.

A VLOOKUP formula has three parts. Part one is the cell where you find the text or number that will be looked for in the first column of your lookup table. Part two is the range where your lookup table is located. Part three is the column of information that contains the information you want to display if a match is found. Lookup Tables will have many rows of information, and will contain 2 or more columns.

### Tasks

*Build the Lists Worksheet*

Select the Lists tab.

Practice Sorting Lists of Data

1.  Highlight cells A16:B25. From the Data menu, Select Sort. Sort by Price and Descending.

2.  Highlight the same area. Use the A/Z icon to re-sort the list in alphabetical order.

3.  Highlight the same area. Copy it. Click on cell D16. From the Edit menu, select Paste Special. Check Transpose. Click OK. Press Escape.

4.  Highlight cells D16:M17. From the Edit menu, select Clear and All. You can use this menu to clear formats.

## Study the County Look-Up Table

The County Table will be used with VLOOKUP functions to find values based on the county you specify in the Invoice worksheet. The first column in VLookUp tables must be sorted alphabetically, A–Z.

Examine the function in cell B13 of the Lists worksheet: =VLOOKUP (Invoice!B8, A5:D10 , 2) The first part of this function tells Excel where to find the name of the County - in cell B8 in the Invoice worksheet. The middle part of the function tells Excel where to find a table that stores information about counties – The range A5 to D10 in this worksheet. The third part of the function tells Excel which column in the table contains the information you want to display in this cell.

How it works: If the user enters Monterey in cell B8 of the Invoice worksheet, Excel will look in the first column of the Counties table to find a matching entry. If it finds a match, it will look in the row that contains the match, and go to column 2. The information in that column will be displayed in the cell containing the VLookUp formula.

Formulas in the Invoice worksheet will pull data from cells B13, C13, and D13 in the Lists worksheet. This data will change whenever the name of the county in cell B8 of the Invoice worksheet changes.

## Build the Invoice Worksheet

**Enter a function to automatically put a date into your invoice.**

1. In cell D3 enter this formula =today(). Make sure there are no spaces between the parentheses.

**Apply special number formatting.**

2. Select cell B9 on the Invoices worksheet. Press Ctrl + 1. Select the Number tab. Choose the Category "Special" and the Type "Phone Number."

**Create a pull-down list of county names.**

3. Select cell F4. Enter this formula =Lists!A5. Copy this formula down into cells F5 to F9.

4. Select cell B8. From the Data menu, select Validation and the Settings tab. For the "Allow" criteria choose List. Click in the Source box. Use your mouse to highlight cells F4:F9. Click OK.

**Create a second pull-down list to show menu items.**

5. In cell F13, enter the formula =Lists!A17. Copy the formula down into cells F14 to F21.

**Apply the menu items pull-down list to multiple cells.**

6. Select cells B13 to B21. From the Data menu, select Data Validation and the Settings tab. For the "Allow" criteria choose List. Click in the Source box. Use your mouse to highlight cells F13:F21. Click OK.

**Use a lookup function to match prices with menu items.**

7. In cell C13, enter the formula =VLOOKUP(B13,Lists!A$17:B$25,2). This function will take the food item entered in cell B13, compare it to the table found in the Lists worksheet, and report back with the menu price found in column 2.

8. Copy the formula down into cells C14 through C21.

**Use an IF statement to calculate the minimum order fee.**

9.   In cell D23, enter this formula =IF(D22>10,0,10-D22).

**Get the sales tax rate for your county (from the look up table on the Lists tab).**

10.   In cell C25 enter this formula =Lists!B13.

**Use an IF statement to calculate the delivery fee.**

11.   In cell D26 enter this formula =IF(D24>50,0,C26).

Cell C26 shows the delivery fee for the county specified in cell B8.

Excel found this in the third column of the County Table using VLookUp.

**Find the total of the invoice.**

12.   In cell D27 enter this formula = SUM(D24:D26).

**Create a link to MapQuest for your driver to use.**

13.   In cell A31, type in www.mapquest.com. This automatically formats as a web-link.

Save the file on the desktop as InvoiceTemplate.

Enter some test data into the invoice form.

1.   Enter data into the customer area.

2.   Enter a sample order in cells A13 to A16. Change the order to see how it affects the total bill.

3.   Change the county (cell B8) and see what happens to the taxes, delivery fee and travel time.

# CHAPTER 7

# PowerPoint for Office XP

## PowerPoint Notes

### Default Settings

From the Tools menu, select Customize and find the Options tab. Turn on these options:

- Show Standard and Formatting toolbars on two rows.
- Always show full menus.
- Show ScreenTips on toolbars.
- Show Shortcut keys in ScreenTips.

### A PowerPoint Presentation Consists of Slides

Slides contain formatted text in outline form. You can also add pictures, clip art, charts, sound, and video. Templates can be used for slide background designs and formatting. Slides are dynamic, using animation effects and transitions to create movement.

PowerPoint is a visual medium, so show ideas with graphics instead of text. Use handouts for any complex written material.

### Creating a New Presentation

If it isn't already displayed, turn on the New Presentation Task Pane from the View menu. The task pane has a pull down selection menu at the upper right. Select New Presentation. If you start a new presentation, you can select a preformatted design, or a blank design. The AutoContent Wizard creates generic formats that students can adapt for their classroom presentations.

### View Options

PowerPoint has three different views: Normal, Slide Sorter and Slide Show. The Task Pane is a separate window. It can be displayed in both the normal and slide sorter views.

*Normal*—combines Slide, Outline, and Notes views with the Task Pane. The windows can be resized by clicking and dragging. Use the Notes area to add details for the lecturer or for handouts. Notes only appear in the slide show if you choose to turn them on.

*Slide Sorter*—shows multiple slides. You can insert or delete slides and use click and drag to reorder slides. You can apply design schemes, add animation and transition effects and create summary slides in this view.

*Slide Show*—shows the slides on the display device.

### New Slides

From Insert menu select New Slide, or use the new slide icon on the formatting toolbar, or press Ctrl + M. The Slide Layout Pane opens. Select a layout. Layouts can be changed in existing slides. Select the slide and open the Slide Layout Pane. Select a layout and click OK.

### Slide Layouts

Layouts control the format of the slide. The three layout types are "Text" for text; "Content" for graphics; and "Other" for non-text and non-graphic elements.

#### Text Slides

One type of text slide is a *Title slide*. The Title slide has this structure:

> Title -
>
> Author -

Another type of text slide is an Information slide. It has a bullet point structure. The bullet points can be turned on and off using the toolbar icon.

#### Content Slides

"Content" layouts hold graphics without any text.

"Text and Content" layouts contain placeholders that you will replace with text, and with pictures, clip art, charts, or graphs. To insert graphics into a 'Content slide' select the placeholder. Select the type of graphic from the set of insertion icons. Find your graphic, and insert it. You can click and drag the formatting placeholders.

#### Other Slides

"Other" layouts are specific to a particular type of graphic. Select a layout that matches the type of information needed on the slide. To insert Graphics into an 'Other' slide, click on the icon.

### Creating and Editing a Slide

Create a slide and select (or change) its layout (see above). Type in new text, format the text, add graphics if desired. You can use any of the standard formatting options available in Word, including changing the font color. The Drawing toolbar options also work in PowerPoint.

To alter the level of bullet points in text slides, use the decrease indent icon and increase indent icons, or use the TAB and SHIFT + TAB keys.

### To Create a Summary Slide

A *Summary Slide* is a computer generated slide that lists the titles of the other slides. Create it last, after the other slides have been created and have titles. From the Slide Sorter View select all (*Ctrl + A*) of the slides. Click the Summary Slide Button on the Slide Show toolbar. (*Alt-Shift-S also works*) Presto! Now click and drag the summary slide to its desired location in the presentation.

You can make a summary for a subset of slides. Hold down Ctrl while selecting the slides to be included in the summary slide then follow the above steps.

### *Spicing Up the Presentation—Adding Content*

#### Using the Slide Master

From the View menu select Master, then Slide Master. Changes to the slide master's format will apply to all slides; you can change backgrounds, font sizes and font types. If you copy a logo, graphic, or picture into the Title area of the Master it will appear on every slide. After you have made your changes, select "Close Slide Master" on the Slide Master toolbar.

*Adding Slide Numbers, Date, and Time:* From the View menu, Header and Footer submenu. Select Date and Time Update automatically. Choose a Date & Time format. Select "slide numbers." Select "Apply to all."

*Design Templates:* From the Format menu, Select Slide Design. The Slide Design Pane opens. Find a template you like; they are listed in alphabetical order. Select the slides you want the design applied to. Now click on the right side of the design you want to apply. This opens a box that gives you the option to apply to selected slides or apply to all slides. You can use several templates within a presentation. You can remove designs by applying the "default design" template.

*You can add color and fill effects.* Right-click in the slide's background area. Select background. Use the pull down menu in the background fill section. *Color Schemes* changes the color combinations used for the design you have already applied to a slide or group of slides.

*Adding an Excel Chart or Worksheet:* Insert menu, Object submenu. Select the type of object from the list. Click Create from file. Locate the required file, click OK. Click outside the chart to return to PowerPoint.

*Adding Sounds or Movies:* Use the Insert menu, Movies and Sounds submenu. Choose something from the clip organizer. Movies should be .mpg or .avi files. You can insert a button icon to play the movie or sound when the icon is clicked. You can use the Custom Animation Task Pane to set the sound to loop, or to play for one or more slides.

*Adding a hyperlink:* Insert a textbox. Right-click and select Add Text. Type in a phrase describing the link. Right click and select Hyperlink. Enter the URL. The link will be active in Slide Show view.

*Adding graphics:* The Word Drawing toolbar also works in PowerPoint. You can insert pictures, Word Art, and Clip Art. Use Ctrl + the arrow keys to fine tune placement.

*Simultaneously Resizing multiple objects:* Hold down the Ctrl + key and click on several graphics (you can include text). Click on a single graphic and use the sizing handles to resize it. The other objects will simultaneously adjust their size.

### *Spicing up the Presentation—Adding Motion*

*Transitions* control how slides replace each other. From Normal or Slide Sorter View, select a slide (or group of slides) and right click. Select Slide Transition. The Slide Transition Pane appears. Follow the prompts from top to bottom. First, select a transition effect and observe how it looks by watching the sample area. Alter its speed if desired, then set it to change automatically or manually. You'll need to insert a time for the delay period if you select automatically. You can then apply the transition effect to the slide master, to all slides, or to a selected slide or slides. If you make a mistake, there is a no-transitions option as one of the effects. This clears any transitions you have selected.

*Animation Effects* control the way bullet points and objects appear on-screen. From the Slide Sorter View open the Slide Design-Animation Schemes Pane. Highlight the slide(s) you want to add animation to. Select an animation effect and observe how it looks by watching the slide in the sample area. Note, there are different categories of animation effects: subtle, moderate, and exciting. You can apply the animation effect to all slides, or apply it to the selected slide or slides. While this pane is open, you can highlight additional slides and apply different animation effects to those slides. If you make a mistake, there is a no-animation option as one of the effects. This clears animations you have added to the selected slide(s). Slides with animation or transitions show a small star underneath them in Slide Sorter View.

### Animating Graphics

Open the Custom Animation Task Pane. Select a graphic element within the slide. Add an effect. Repeat with each graphic element. Press the play button when finished to review the animation sequence.

*To change the order of effects:* Open the custom animation Task Pane. Click on the effect you want to move. Select the Reorder up or down arrow at the bottom of the task pane.

*To change the timing of effects:* On the custom animation task pane, you can set the speed of the effect.

*To change the order in which overlapping graphics appear:* Select a graphic. On the Drawing toolbar, select Draw then select Order.

*To show effects simultaneously:* In the Custom Animation Task Pane, hold down Ctrl while selecting the effects you want to use together. In the Start box, select With Previous.

*To show effects together in sequences:* In the Custom Animation Task Pane select the effects you want to use together. In the Start box, select After Previous.

*Animated clip art* can be added to content slides. After creating a content slide, you'll see a set of icons in the frame. Click on the Insert Media Clip icon. Type a word into the search box. Animated objects have a small gold star in the corner. Click on the clip art to insert it.

*To create an endless loop:* From the Slide Show menu, choose Set Up Show. In the Dialog box, check Loop continuously until Esc. In the Transitions pane set the timer. Apply to all slides.

*To add movement buttons* to a presentation use the Slide Show menu, Action Buttons submenu.

### Showing the Presentation

Press F5 to begin the show.

*To move to next slide:* Page Down, N, left click with Mouse, or use the down arrow key.

*To move to previous slide:* Page Up, or P, or use the up-arrow key.

*To jump directly to a slide:* Type in the slide number and press enter, or right click and choose a slide from the pull down menu.

*To move to the first or last slide:* Press the Home or End key.

*To set a timer to display the slides:* See Transition Effects and Animation Effects.

*To use the mouse as a pen:* Right click during the show and select Pointer Options.

*To temporarily show a blank screen:* Press Shift-B or period for a black background, Shift-W or comma for a white one. Repeating returns to the slide show.

*To end a slide show:* Press Escape.

### Printing Slides and Lecture Notes

*To show speaker notes on your PC, without projecting them:* You can view speaker notes at any time during a broadcast by right-clicking any slide, and then clicking Screen and then Speaker Notes. Extra hardware must be installed to show notes on the PC and not on the display.

*To print handouts:* From the File menu, Print submenu, set Print What to 'handouts.' You can change the number of slides printed per page. Frame Slides should be checked. Click OK.

*Printing PowerPoint to Word for student to use in note taking:* Choose File, then Send to, then select Microsoft Word. This lets you create a copy of the presentation with spaces for note-taking.

### Saving the PowerPoint Presentation

PowerPoint files can get quite large. Simply renaming the file when you save it helps to shrink the file, sometimes significantly.

# PowerPoint Assignment

**Follow the instructions below to create 4 slides (or more, if you feel creative) about a topic that interests you. After you create your presentation, use the summary slide feature to generate a summary slide. The slides must be created for this class; do not submit slides you created for a presentation to another class.**

For more information and for examples of student work, go to *www.cob.sjsu.edu/splane_m/Index3.htm*

1.  Create a title slide that will contain your name, your presentation topic, and your section number.

2.  Use a different text size and font for each of the three lines.

3.  The second slide should contain a brief outline of your presentation. You should have at least one example of a two level indentation. (Hint: Use the tab key or the indent icon.)

4.  The third slide should contain an image obtained from the Clip Art library, with a text description.

5.  The fourth slide should contain additional text information and a graphic. Either create something from the Drawing toolbar or import a picture.

6.  Each slide must have a title as well as the contents listed above. Add titles if you haven't already done so.

7.  Create a summary slide—use the summary slide feature.

    Create this slide last, after you have completed the other slides. The icon for creating summary slides is on the toolbar in the Slide Sorter View. You must select some slides before this icon becomes active. You must use text, not Word Art, in the title areas of the slides.

8.  Move the summary slide to the end of the presentation.

9.  Add the date, the time, and slide numbers to the slides.

    This is a Footer, so look on the View menu. You can select a combination date and time setting from a pull-down list in the dialog box.

10. Add a background color, or apply a design template, to the slides.

11. Add transition effects to the slides.

12. Add animation effects to the slides.

13. Add automatic slide transitions so each slide is displayed automatically without requiring any mouse clicks. The presentation should not exceed two minutes.

14. Add a continuous loop setting.

# Supplemental Material—Presentation Advice

## Structuring Your Talk

Preparing a talk always takes far longer than you anticipate. **Start early!**

- Write a clear statement of the problem and its importance.
- Research. Collect material which may relate to the topic.
- Tell a story in a logical sequence.
- Stick to the key concepts. Avoid description of specifics and unnecessary details.
- If you are making a series of points, organize them from the most to the least important. The less important points can be skipped if you run short of time.
- Keep your sentences short, about 10–20 words each is ideal. This is the way people usually talk.
- Strive for clarity. Are these the best words for making your point? Are they unambiguous? Are you using unfamiliar jargon or acronyms?

## Preparing Your Slides

- Presentation Design
  - Don't overload your slides with too much text or data.
  - FOCUS. In general, using a few powerful slides is the aim.
  - Let the picture or graphic tell the story. Avoid text.
  - Type key words in the PowerPoint Notes area listing what to say when displaying the slide. The notes are printable.
  - Number your slides and give them a title.
  - Use the "summary slide" feature in Slide Sorter View to prepare an Agenda or Table of Contents slide.
  - Prepare a company logo slide for your presentation.
  - You can add a logo and other graphics to every slide using the slide master feature.
  - Proofread everything, including visuals and numbers.
  - Keep "like" topics together.
  - Strive for similar line lengths for text.
- Visual elements
  - A font size of 28 to 34 with a bold font is recommended for subtitles. The title default size is 44. Use a sans serif font for titles.
  - Use clear, simple visuals. Don't confuse the audience.
  - Use contrast: light on dark or dark on light.
  - Graphics should make a key concept clearer.
  - Place your graphics in a similar location within each screen.

- The Drawing toolbar is extremely useful. You can:
  - Insert clip art.
  - Insert pictures.
  - Use Word Art.
  - Use text boxes.
  - Insert charts and diagrams.
  - Insert arrows, banners, and thought balloons.
- To temporarily clear the screen, press W or B during the presentation. Press Enter to resume the presentation.

- Text
  - Font size must be large enough to be easily read. Size 28 to 34 with a bold font is recommended.
  - It is distracting if you use too wide a variety of fonts.
    - Unusual fonts may not display as you intended.
  - Overuse of text is a common mistake.
    - Too much text makes the slide unreadable. You may just as well show a blank slide. Stick to a few key words.
    - If your audience is reading the slides they are not paying attention to you. If possible, make your point with graphics instead of text.
    - You can use Word Art, or a clip art image of a sign, to convey text in a more interesting way.

- Numbers
  - Numbers are usually confusing to the audience. Use as few as possible and allow extra time for the audience to do the math.
  - Numbers should never be ultra precise:
    - "Anticipated Revenues of $660,101.83" looks silly. Are your numbers that accurate? Just say $660 thousand.
    - "The Break Even Point is 1048.17 units." Are you selling fractions of a Unit?
    - Don't show pennies. Cost per unit is about the only time you would need to show pennies.
  - If you have more than 12–15 numbers on a slide, that's probably too many.
  - Using only one number per sentence helps the audience absorb the data.

- Statistics
  - Use the same scale for numbers on a slide. Don't compare thousands to millions.
  - When using sales data, stick to a single market in the presentation. Worldwide sales, domestic sales, industry sales, company sales, divisional sales, or sales to a specific market segment are all different scales. They should not be mixed.
  - Cite your source on the same slide as the statistic, using a smaller size font.

- Charts
  - Charts need to be clearly labeled. You can make more interesting charts by adding elements from the Drawing toolbar.

- Numbers in tables are both hard to see and to understand. There is usually a better way to present your numerical data than with columns and rows of numbers. Get creative!
- PowerPoint deletes portions of charts and worksheets that are imported from Excel, keeping only the leftmost 5.5 inches. Plan ahead.

- Backgrounds
  - Backgrounds should never distract from the presentation.
  - Using the default white background is hard on the viewer's eyes. You can easily add a design style or a color to the background.
  - Backgrounds that are light colored with dark text, or vice versa, look good. A dark background with white font reduces glare. It is difficult to see text on multi-colored backgrounds.
  - Colors appear lighter when projected. Pale colors often appear as white.
  - Consistent backgrounds add to a professional appearance.
  - For a long presentation, you may want to change background designs when shifting to a new topic.

- Excitement
  - Slides for business presentations should be dull! You don't want to distract the audience.
  - Sounds and transition effects can be annoying. Use sparingly.
  - Animation effects can be interesting when used in moderation.
    - Too much animation is distracting.
    - Consider using animated clip art.
    - Consider using custom animation.
  - You can insert video and audio clips into PowerPoint.
  - You can also insert hyperlinks.

## *Hints for Efficient Practice*

- Timing—Practicing Your Presentation
  - Talk through your presentation to see how much time you use for each slide.
  - Set the automatic slide transition to the amount of time you want to spend discussing each slide.
  - Are you using the right amount of time per slide? Decide which slides or comments need alteration to make your presentation smoother.
  - Change the automatic slide transition settings for individual slides to fit the amount of time needed for that slide and practice again. Are you still within the time limit?
  - Decide if you want to remove the automatic slide transition feature before giving the presentation.

- Content
  - Make a list of key words/concepts for each slide.
  - Read through the list before you begin.
  - Don't attempt to memorize your text.

- Your words will probably be different each time you practice.

- Think about the ideas, and your words will follow naturally.

### Delivering Your Talk

- Pre-Talk Preparation

  - Plan to get there a few minutes early to set up and test the equipment.

  - Dress appropriately for your audience.

  - Turn off your cell phone.

  - Handouts:

    - Edward Tufte, the leading expert on visual presentation techniques, advises speakers to always prepare a handout when giving a PowerPoint presentation.

    - Make about 10% more handouts than you expect to use.

    - Distribute handouts at the beginning of your talk.

- Opening

  - Jump right in and get to the point.

  - Give your rehearsed opening statement; don't improvise at the last moment.

  - Use the opening to catch the interest and attention of the audience.

  - Briefly state the problem or topic you will be discussing.

  - Briefly summarize your main theme for an idea or solution.

- Speaking

  - Talk at a natural, moderate rate of speech.

  - Project your voice.

  - Speak clearly and distinctly.

  - Repeat critical information.

  - Pause briefly to give your audience time to digest the information on each new slide.

  - Don't read the slides aloud. Your audience can read them far faster than you can talk.

- Body Language

  - Keep your eyes on the audience.

  - Use natural gestures.

  - Don't turn your back to the audience.

  - Don't hide behind the lectern.

  - Avoid looking at your notes. Only use them as reference points to keep you on track. Talk, don't read.

- Questions

  - Always leave time for a few questions at the end of the talk.

  - If you allow questions during the talk, the presentation time will be about 25% longer than the practice time.

- You can jump directly to a slide by typing its number or by right-clicking during the presentation and choosing from the slide titles.

  - Relax. If you've done the research you can easily answer most questions.

  - Some questions are too specific or personal. Politely refuse to answer.

  - If you can't answer a question, say so. Don't apologize. "I don't have that information. I'll try to find out for you."

- Length

  - To end on time, you must PRACTICE!

  - When practicing, try to end early. You need to allow time for audience interruptions and questions.

- Demeanor

  - Show some enthusiasm. Nobody wants to listen to a dull presentation. On the other hand, don't overdo it. Nobody talks and gestures like a maniac in real life. How would you explain your ideas to a friend?

  - Involve your audience. Ask questions, make eye contact, use humor.

  - Don't get distracted by audience noises or movements.

  - You'll forget a minor point or two. Everybody does.

  - If you temporarily lose your train of thought, you can gain time to recover by asking if the audience has any questions.

- Conclusion

  - Close the sale.

  - Concisely summarize your key concepts and the main ideas of your presentation.

  - Resist the temptation to add a few last impromptu words.

  - End your talk with the summary statement or question you have prepared. What do you want them to do? What do you want them to remember?

  - Consider alternatives to "Questions?" for your closing slide. A summary of your key points, a cartoon, a team logo, or a company logo may be stronger.

# CHAPTER 8

# Internet Explorer

This course assumes students are familiar with using a browser. Here are some tips that may be useful.

**To expand or shrink the display:** This hides or displays the toolbars. Press F11.

**To create a picture of the display screen:** Press the Print Screen key (next to F12 on most keyboards). The image is stored on the clipboard. Now paste it into Word or another Office application. Select the image and modify it using the Format menu, Picture submenu.

**To create a picture of the active window:** Hold down ALT or Ctrl + and press the Print Screen key (next to F12 on most keyboards.) The image is stored on the clipboard. Now paste it into Word or another Office application. Select the image and modify it using the Format menu, Picture submenu.

**To copy a picture from a webpage:** Right-click on the picture. Select Copy. Open an Office application and choose paste. Note: Pressing Ctrl + V is a shortcut method for pasting.

**To look for a word on a webpage:** Press Ctrl + F.

**To return to your home page:** Hold down Alt and Home.

**To refresh the current webpage:** Press F5.

**To open a link in a new window:** Press Shift when clicking on the link.

**To move between viewed web pages:** Press Backspace or press ALT plus the left arrow to move backward. Press ALT plus the right arrow to move forward.

**To go to the top of a web page:** Press the Home key.

**To go to the end of a web page:** Press the End key.

**To quickly scroll in a web page:** Put the cursor in the scrollbar at the estimated location of where you want to be in the web page. Right click. Click on Scroll Here.

**To quickly access a .com site:** Type the words of the site's name in the Address bar. Omit the http, www, and .com portions. Press Ctrl + ENTER.

**To search from the Address bar:** Type go, find, or ? followed by a word or phrase, and then press ENTER. Or, type Google and Press Ctrl + ENTER.

**To look up a definition:** Type *Define:* in the address bar, followed by the word.

**To copy a table from the web into Excel:** Highlight the data and copy it. In Excel, choose an empty sheet. Ctrl + A. Paste. Click OK to clear the error message.

**To remove formatting when pasting from a webpage into Word:** Use Paste Special and select an Unformatted or a Rich Text Format.